CRASHPROOF PROSPERITY

BECOMING WEALTHY IN THE AGE OF RISK

BY
KIP HERRIAGE

VERTICAL RESEARCH ADVISORY
HOUSTON, TEXAS USA

Vertical Research Advisory
1600 Highway 6, Suite 360
Sugar Land, TX 77478 USA

For information about special discounts for bulk purchases or to book the author
for live speaking engagements, please contact Vertical Research Advisory at
1-832-532-7655.

Editor: Tim McDonnell
Cover/Text design: Eve Marie Vrla/Eve Vrla Design, Ltd.

First printing, January, 2011
ISBN: 978-0-578-07310-1 (pbk)

Herriage, Kip
CRASHPROOF PROSPERITY
Becoming Wealthy in the Age of Risk

Printed in the United States of America

DEDICATION

This book is dedicated to the priceless people who are my
"why" – the value and meaning of my life – my beautiful wife,
Cindy and two my amazing sons, Tyler and Sam.
You are my world and I am blessed to be a part of yours.

SPECIAL THANKS

My acknowledgements wouldn't be complete without
expressing deep gratitude to my editor and lead researcher,
Tim McDonnell. Tim, you have the very rare gift of helping
others find their voice and place it into the written word. Not
many can say that they are in fact doing what they were born
to do, but this statement absolutely applies to you.
Thank you for making this book a reality!

CONTENTS

8

INTRODUCTION
EVERYTHING'S
CONNECTED

They haven't agreed on what it is or what to call it yet, but the folks in the lab coats on the fringes of science now know that there's an invisible energy field that connects everything in the universe. Every object you think of as real – you, me, this book, everyone you know, your possessions and even the space you occupy right now – is part of it. Now, here's the really interesting part. High-energy physics experiments have proven beyond any doubt that it's possible to influence the behavior of the subatomic waves and particles that make up everything *simply by observing them.* If that doesn't blow your mind, try this one on for size. Living cells taken from human lab volunteers showed measurable electrical responses to things the cell donors were doing, even when the test subjects and the cell samples were not located in the same room – *and even before the test subject had actually performed the intended action.*

If the world we know and everything in it responds to the same underlying vibrations (of which our own thoughts and intentions are an inseparable part), can you begin to see why every choice we make is so important? At the subatomic level, the universe really doesn't make any meaningful distinction between an object in your hand, one that's light years away, or one that doesn't even exist yet in the physical world. If that's true (and the preponderance of scientific evidence says it is), then the relevance of this concept to the global economic crisis we're all facing today begins to become clear. We no longer have the luxury of assuming that what happens in other countries will not impact our well being or that our actions will not affect other economies around the world. As the leaders of the world's governmental and financial institutions have proven, it's impossible to manipulate one part of an interdependent system without experiencing consequences in other parts of the system.

This is the underlying theme to what *Crashproof Prosperity* is all about. When you boil it down to its essence, money is simply another form of energy – a representation of intrinsic value that can't be destroyed. It only changes form and direction. What you and I call "the economy" is really nothing more than a model of all the transactions between people exchanging something they value for something they need or want. Since the dawn of civilization, different mediums of exchange have come and gone, from simple barter to precious metals to paper currency, but the true essence of "money" never really goes away, even in a "down" economy. It just changes hands, follows value and flows in new directions.

To help get our heads around the practical implications of these concepts, it's hard to find a more powerful (or entertaining!) illustration than the classic sci-fi thriller *The Matrix*. It's one of my all time favorite movies and I quote it a lot. As the story unfolds, a young computer hacker meets a mysterious band of rebels who awaken him from a false perception of reality and call him to battle against the dark forces that control it. The adventurers in *The Matrix* responded to a choice between lifelong bondage in an artificial comfort zone or the freedom of seeing the real world on the other side of the illusion.

Since 2005, when Karl Bessey and I formed Wealth Masters International, we have been offering people the same choice. In an eerie, real-life parallel to *The Matrix*, the world you and I live in is also running on two completely separate operating systems – one for the independently minded "new paradigm" and the other for the masses operating in the "old paradigm," or the *sheeple* as I refer to them. There's a profit system for entrepreneurs and a wage system for workers. The only way to attain any kind of lasting prosperity is to leave the illusion of the old paradigm and move into the reality of the new paradigm.

Sadly, most people don't even realize they have a choice. The economic crisis that's unfolding now is scaring the heck out of a lot of people. If it hasn't already had an impact on you or someone you know, the fallout is going to affect virtually everyone, and it's almost certain that the economy will only get worse from here. Right now the average person is caught like a deer in the headlights, and while that's completely understandable given the weak economy, this is exactly the wrong time to stand pat. 99%

of the population is waiting for a turnaround in the economy, the stock market, and the real estate market because we've become accustomed to the "boom and bust" cycle of the old paradigm. In the past, during a typical recession, the conventional wisdom of holding on to what you had and waiting for a recovery made sense. Here's the problem with that logic now – it's highly likely that there won't be any real recovery in the global economy for several more years. We're going through a massive deleveraging process, both at home and abroad, and until this cycle completes itself it will be impossible for a sustained recovery to begin.

Yet, true to the dual system we live under, the so-called "experts" continue to feed the worst possible advice to people trapped in the old paradigm, while the small percentage of those embracing the new paradigm continue to see through the smokescreen. Think about it this way – our so-called leaders failed to predict the economic downturn we're in today, so why should we trust them with our hard-earned money going forward? I can guarantee you that these individuals don't know how far down the rabbit hole we're going to go, which sectors of the economy will be hit the hardest, or how the economies of other nations will react. People are finally beginning to question the policies and ethics of central banks, our fiat currency system, Washington, Wall Street and Corporate America and wondering how they could have ever allowed this mess to happen in the first place. This global awakening is the beginning of quantifiable change.

Most people spend so much time focusing on the recession/depression that they can easily lose sight of the fact that we're witnessing the very early innings of the greatest wealth transfer in history. Make no mistake about it – this wealth shift has already begun and you're making a choice whether you know it or not. You've either decided to take advantage of this massive, never-before-seen movement of wealth, or you've decided to ignore the subject. But either way, you *have* made a choice. Let me put it this way – if you're sick and tired of being sick and tired – if you're fed up with worrying about your finances and your future – and if you're stone cold serious about having an investment account with at least seven figures, then I'm happy to tell you that you do have an alternative.

This is why it's up to you to look behind the "matrix" and become informed on the real issues at hand. It's time to become self-empowered and begin making decisions based on your own knowledge and instincts. No one cares more about your financial future than you! In the midst of great turmoil there's always great opportunity, but you need the clarity to recognize it and the courage to move in a different direction from the masses. Entrepreneurs thrive in this kind of environment and you can, too. This is exactly why I began publishing the Vertical Research Advisory investment newsletter in 2002 and why we created Wealth Masters International in 2005 – to ultimately help millions to become self-reliant and achieve more than they ever thought possible. It's also why I decided to publish *Crashproof Prosperity* in this year – after having written enough material to fill at least five books from 2005 on, the chain of events occurring today mandated it. You're about to discover why there's never been a more urgent moment in history to arm yourself with information and then act on it – I believe your personal and financial destiny depends on it.

Kip Herriage
January 2011
Sugar Land, Texas

CHAPTER ONE
WHAT'S PAST
IS PROLOGUE

The ideas I'm going to present to you in this book are intended to shake the outdated assumptions and beliefs you've held about the way the financial world operates. My objective is not to give you an academic overview of economics – there are plenty of good history and theory books already out there and before we're done, I'll recommend a couple of them for you. What I'm giving you here is a lot like the safety briefing you get before any commercial airline flight – it's not medical training or aviation science – just the quick facts you need to survive an emergency. These are my observations, based on my own years of success on Wall Street as well as the work of a handful of some of the brightest, most integrity-driven independent thinkers in the world of finance today. Be prepared to be challenged, because while these ideas are based on pure common sense, most of them run in direct opposition to what you've been led to believe about our countries, as well as our world's, economic policies and financial institutions.

The old paradigm simply isn't working anymore. For those who are not prepared, it saddens me to say that the consequences are going to be disastrous. For others who act quickly to put the right protective measures in place, there's still a little time left to not only survive the inevitable collapse of a broken system, but to actually profit from the opportunities that always accompany every calamity. Like many people, your own instincts and common sense have probably been telling you that there's a strange disconnect between the vague and benign economic reports you keep hearing in the media and the reality of our current global economic situation. As with any puzzle, without key pieces of information and the right frame of reference, it's going to be virtually impossible for you to connect the dots correctly. To set the stage for some of what we're going to be talking about in the pages ahead, consider just a few of the financial predictions I've published over the last few years.

In 2002, I recommended gold at $290/oz (now over $1,400/oz) and silver at $4.75/oz (now over $30/oz), based on the bear market and future implosion of the US dollar. In 2003 I called China "the Chinese Miracle" and successfully recommended a number of Chinese investments that delivered huge returns. In 2005 I began warning everyone about the coming bankruptcy of the US, the emerging subprime lending crisis, and the real estate bubble and crash. In September, 2008 I advised investors to start selling stocks and shorting the stock market just weeks before the market plummeted 40%. In December, 2008 I recommended mining stocks at the market low, resulting in returns of several hundred to over 1000%.

Folks, there's a documented audit trail proving that, as far back as the "dot-bomb" bust in the technology sector in 2000, I've accurately called every one of these events in advance. Oh, maybe not to the day or decimal, but certainly in substance and in sequence, the signs were all there for anyone with the experience and insight to read and act on them. Since 2002 I have been on the right side of individual investment recommendations to the tune of 90% plus through my Vertical Research Advisory (VRA) newsletter, and if anyone has a better track record in the newsletter business I have yet to meet them. If you did not read my work and were not one of the people who saw it coming, don't feel bad. You really weren't supposed to know, and that's another part of what *Crashproof Prosperity* is all about. Only a few voices raised any concern about impending collapse in these and other key areas, and I can tell you that virtually none of them were in positions of leadership over our country's economic policies and financial institutions. So how was I able to do it and what does it mean to all of us today? That part of the story requires just a little bit of background, so bear with me. I promise you that by the end of this book, you'll see why it's all relevant. Everything really is connected.

In the book *Two Roads, One Journey* that Karl and I wrote December 2009, several chapters covered my upbringing and

18

professional background, so I'm not going to spend a lot of time on those things here. I will touch briefly on some of my early experiences on Wall Street and a few of my first exposures to entrepreneurship, however, so that you can look for parallels in your own life. Part of what *Crashproof Prosperity* is all about is learning to recognize the seeds of prosperity that are all around you. Those who have learned how to create lasting abundance in their lives are the ones who have trained themselves to discern the truth about a situation, see the opportunity in it and then act on it with purpose. That's why I'm giving you this information – so that you can learn to take charge of your own financial destiny, rather than leaving it in the hands of government "rescuers" who, quite frankly, are never going to come to your aid. In order to get through this, we're going to have to learn how to save ourselves. People may develop these skills of observation and action in their own way and at their own pace, but I don't know a single self-made millionaire who has not mastered them and made them a habit of life. We'll go deeper into these success habits and more in a later chapter.

By May of 1999 I had been a money manager and VP for 15 years and enjoying the rewards of a long and successful career run. I didn't know it at the time but I was on my way to my last Wall Street conference. Each year the company took its top executives to an annual week-long getaway, families and all. This particular conference was at the lavish Boca Raton Resort in Florida and they treated us like royalty. My wife, Cindy and my two sons Tyler and Sam were there as well and having a great time. I should have felt like I was on top of the world. After all, I had been in the business a long while and had built an income that allowed me to provide my family with financial security and a seemingly great lifestyle.

But I wasn't happy. In fact, I was miserable, but I didn't understand why at first. For those that have read *Two Roads, One Journey*, you know that I come from a lower middle class family that sometimes didn't have enough money to eat three *real* meals a day. For several years we lived in a mobile home and my parents fought about money pretty much constantly until they eventually divorced when I was 13. This chronic sense of lack, and the stress that came along with it, became my primary motivation to make money — and lots of it. I pushed myself all the way through high school in hopes of breaking the cycle of scarcity I'd grown up with, working first at McDonalds, then Wal-Mart. I also worked full-time while putting myself through college, where I became the first ever two-term President of the Interfraternity Council and the campus rep for Adolph Coors (and yes, that was a fun job). After college I became a financial advisor — something I had dreamed of and clearly visualized for years — and while still in my twenties was promoted to Vice President of Private and Corporate accounts with global leader Oppenheimer. By the age of 37 I was managing $70 million, had earned my own millions, had two amazing sons with Cindy, and should have been well on my way to enjoying the fruits of my labor. Based on my blueprint for success (as I understood it at the time) I should have been extremely happy.

My initial wake-up call came when I watched the first investment firm I worked for implode because of its own internal conflicts, plus the mismanagement of an Initial Public Offering (IPO) of a mortgage derivatives fund, brought to us by our new hotshot MBA CEO out of some Ivy League business school. That one single investment brought down a 100-year-old firm and lost our investors at least $50 million. This was when $50 million was actually a lot of money, before the current level of dollar printing, or currency inflation kicked in and we added a bunch of zeroes — before we started accepting the idea of trillion dollar deficits and bailouts as "normal."

The firm had been blinded by the upside potential of this mortgage-related, derivatives-based algorithmic program that they felt had been hedged in every way possible and believed would earn the firm millions in fees over the next few years. They were wrong. In less than nine months this one risky move brought the entire firm down. About five years later while at Oppenheimer, I watched two of the red hot IPO opportunities the company was pushing file for bankruptcy within a single year. This time the investors took a hit of well over $100 million dollars for following chapter and verse of the firm's official (but very carefully worded) marketing position. In both instances, no one was fired and no one went to jail. No one was forced to take responsibility. Incredible.

As I sat in our Boca Resort suite on that beautiful spring day in 1999, reflecting back on these early lessons and other events, it started to dawn on me just how unhappy I really was. Between my travels, a 60+ hour workweek and a two-hour daily commute, I was hardly ever home. My family deserved a better father and spouse, and I deserved to enjoy life and my chosen profession. The hard truth was that I wasn't enjoying my profession. Although I had either met or exceeded virtually every material goal I'd ever set for myself since high school, a part of me knew that something was missing. Maybe you've experienced that same strange sense of discontent in your life, too.

My instincts were telling me that the game was rigged – that the commercial and institutional end of the system was not really set up to favor the average consumer's best interests. In the financial advisory capacity where my true passions were, I felt a nagging frustration that I was only able to help a few high-net-worth individuals. That's when I finally realized that I wasn't put on this earth to serve Wall Street – and that maybe I had some gifts that were meant for a higher purpose. Within four months I had left my Wall Street career behind me for good. I had no idea what I would do next, but I knew deep down that something more important was waiting for me. The entrepreneurial spirit inside of me was calling. I now know that everything happens for a reason and that there really are no accidents.

With that idea in mind, hindsight makes it a lot easier for me to understand how I first caught the entrepreneurial spark that inspires me today and what it was that prepared me to be able to interpret market signs as a truly independent financial advisor, not based on industry marketing hype or the cooked statistical books we get from government "experts." Even as a kid growing up near Houston, Texas, I already knew that I wanted to own my own business someday. I started mowing lawns at 10 and loved it. From then on, the idea of working for somebody else never appealed to me compared with the excitement of becoming an entrepreneur. For me, my calling was clear right out of the gate. When I landed that first job as a rookie stockbroker, my first branch manager required us to work 12 hours a day and I was usually the first one in the office and last to leave. I read everything I could get my hands on – of course The Wall Street Journal every day and Barron's each Saturday – and I began to build my investment book library.

The key lessons I learned in those early days were a) the importance of mentors that I could trust, and b) that *nothing* can replace the major investment of time and effort it takes to study and become a true expert in your chosen field. Just because someone claims to be an expert doesn't necessarily mean that they know what they're talking about. I knew from everything I'd read, and from my own early experience, that it was important to be with a known and respected firm so that the brand name would help me attract clients. That's how I found my way to Oppenheimer fairly early in the game. I landed my first multi-million dollar account after my branch manager gave me the inactive accounts file, because no one else wanted to work them. Remember, most of my coworkers were trust fund babies and didn't really need the money. But I was hungry and he knew it. He said, "I'm not sure what you will do with these. These clients have either moved on to other firms or have only a few dollars in their account."

I started calling those old accounts immediately with the expectation that I was going to win back their business, and did it ever work. Within a week a well-known doctor in Houston transferred his seven-figure accounts back to me and I was on my way. From there, I began to take a serious interest in investment banking and venture capital. I began looking for emerging growth companies that wanted to eventually take their companies public. Over the years I helped take seven companies public and we are well on our way to achieving the same goal with Wealth Masters International (WMI). Through all of these experiences, and by closely observing the successes and failures in the market, I learned what it takes to build a quality company that can stand the test of time. To get great results, you have to think outside of the box and make great decisions. It's as simple as that. My friend and trend forecasting pioneer Gerald Celente explains that there's nothing especially mystical about accurately predicting the future. It's all about understanding where we've been so that we can see where we're going.

CHAPTER TWO
CHOICES, CONSEQUENCES, CYCLES

As this book is rolling off the press, every indicator that I follow is flashing bright red. For example, Europe is witnessing the beginning of the end of their common currency, the Euro. This currency collapse will be followed by trillions in new bank losses globally, and cause economic devastation throughout the world. We're already seeing the consequences of staggering national debts that are mathematically impossible to repay in countries like Japan, Spain, Portugal, Ireland and Greece. Meanwhile, institutions like the International Monetary Fund (IMF) and the World Bank continue to pour more "relief" money into these broken economies, further devaluing our baseless global currencies and accelerating the beginnings of hyperinflation. In the United States, trillions in taxpayer funded bailouts and loan guarantees — not to mention the untold trillions spent secretly by the Federal Reserve and central banks globally – have done little to get the economy on its feet again, and in hindsight will be shown to have done nothing more than contribute greatly to the US more than $100 trillion in total US debt. Debt that cannot, and will never be repaid.

This is it. We're officially crossing the line that I've been warning about since the inception of WMI, and prior to that, from the formation of the VRA. Events in the world economy will now begin to unfold one after another in a seemingly uncontrollable fashion. Clueless governments still don't understand that it was their ruinous actions that created a credit infested, fiat currency based, bankrupt world. They didn't learn this lesson from their mistakes in the 1930s and now it's too late to prevent another disturbingly similar "lost decade" this time around. Trust me when I say that they will continue to prescribe the same failed remedies that caused the problem in the first place, specifically, more government bailouts and more printed money. This isn't just my opinion – it's already happening and the consequences are clear. We will soon see hyperinflation, economic misery, and in many parts of the world, social unrest very similar to what we're already seeing in the UK, Greece and France.

Never in history has the world been in a situation where virtually all major industrialized democracies are bankrupt at the same time. And many feel that because there really is no precedent for what will happen in the next few years that our future looks bleak, if not terrifying. Were I still stuck in my old Wall Street mindset, I might share this dark and pessimistic view. Sure,

I'm concerned about what's headed our way, and I'm extremely concerned for those that remain unprepared. However, there is a big flip side to this coin. You see, it's in times just like these where massive wealth is created. For many this concept may be difficult to comprehend, but in all of recorded history, cycles of economic upheaval have always brought with them a new beginning, and through these new beginnings, untold opportunities to build what I call generational wealth — secure, lasting prosperity that can be passed along from one generation to the next. Those who know me from my VRA updates or the Wealth Masters community hear me repeatedly emphasize the fact that more wealth was created coming out of the Great Depression than existed before it began. But how can this be? Doesn't money just disappear when the stock market and the real estate market and the currency markets all collapse? Although this may seem counterintuitive at first, the answer is no. Money doesn't ever really go away, even when economic indicators are at their lowest.

This is where the most important point I can make comes into play. Both money and the energy that binds the universe share a common, fundamental trait. Like energy, money never disappears. And, just as waves and particles of energy remain in a constant flow throughout the universe, perpetually changing into mass and back into energy again, money similarly follows value from place to place, changing hands as it moves from the *ill-informed* to the *well-informed*. This is a big part of what I mean by old paradigm versus new paradigm and why I'm putting such urgency behind getting this information into your hands right now. The economic uncertainty unfolding around us will cause many to be scared and unsure of what their future holds. And while some of you reading this may go through periods where you share those same concerns, the most important thing you can do is to maintain a laser-like focus on the opportunities that exist all around you. You see, entrepreneurs and independent thinkers will be the biggest winners of all in the years to come. When you surround yourself with like-minded visionaries and take responsibility to develop your own critical thinking skills and financial literacy, you'll find that you actually already possess everything you need to survive and thrive.

So, where are we now and how bad are things really getting out there? Well, let's take a quick look back at what our top leaders have been telling us over the past five years. *"FED Chairman Alan Greenspan relaxed about house prices...this is not a bubble of any magnitude,"* reported the Financial Times in 2005. *"Most negatives in housing are probably behind us,"* Greenspan said in October, 2006. *"We believe the effect of the troubles in the subprime sector...will be likely limited,"* said current Fed Chairman Ben Bernanke in March, 2007. *"[It's] not a serious problem...I think it's going to be largely contained,"* added Treasury Secretary Henry Paulson in April, 2007. All you have to do is look objectively at the events taking place all around us to realize that all of these statements were 180 degrees out of phase with the truth.

Now, these same people are telling us that they can save capitalism from itself with trillions in bailouts and that additional "economic stimulus" will be required. For the last 15 years, the US money supply has grown about twice as fast as the Gross Domestic Product (GDP). Meanwhile, Federal government liabilities have grown three times as fast. As a result, the USA now has more financial obligations than assets, making it effectively bankrupt. This year's US government deficit will add about $1.5 trillion to the total. The US trade deficit is about $700 billion. The US bailout plan will probably cost at least $1 trillion more every year for the next 5 years (at minimum). Where will the government get that kind of money? The answer – at some point they won't be able to get it. *Everything* is at risk now – the economy, jobs, basic commodities, survival necessities, housing prices – essentially our entire way of life.

There's a lot more to this story, but before we go on it might be a good idea to stop for a minute and give ourselves a frame of reference. Have you ever noticed how casually our main stream media, government leaders and major financial institutions seem to talk about stimulus packages, bailouts and debts numbering in the trillions? Most people have trouble getting their heads around numbers this big and some experts suggest that our brains aren't even biologically wired to handle them. For starters, a trillion is a one followed by *twelve* zeroes. In US currency, the one hundred dollar bill is the largest denomination in general circulation these days. You'll find Benjamin Franklin's picture on the front and he's guaranteed to make friends and open doors for you wherever he goes. A standard $10,000 bundle of these is about a half inch thick. It'll fit very comfortably in your coat pocket and buy you a pretty exciting weekend in Las Vegas.

Believe it or not, even though it sounds like a lot more money, even a million dollars worth of hundred dollar bills still fits in a large shoebox or a small shopping bag and you can carry it around with you very easily. A hundred million stacked in a cube fits neatly on a standard shipping pallet. A billion dollars takes up eight pallets – still pretty easy to visualize. Are you ready for this? One trillion dollars stacked two pallets high would dwarf a person standing next to it and look a lot like the top secret government warehouse that Indiana Jones' crate disappeared into at the end of *Raiders of the Lost Ark.* Michael Maloney, an acclaimed expert on precious metals and the world banking system does an unforgettable visual presentation on this concept at our live Wealth Masters events and if you ever see it, I guarantee it will have an impact on you.

Not everyone processes information in exactly the same way, so here are a few more quick examples. Texas, the state I live in, takes up about 270,000 square miles. A trillion square miles would equal 3.7 million states the size of Texas. In fact, if you accept the current estimate of 50 billion square miles above sea level, a trillion square miles would actually equal around twenty earth-sized planets. A trillion one dollar bills laid end to end would stretch to the sun and back with a few bucks to spare. If you subtract out the costs of the wars in Iraq and Afghanistan, a trillion dollars would cover *all* of the regular operating costs of the US Department of Defense for two years. By the way, did you know that one of the DoD's biggest single line items is pensions? A trillion dollars would provide roughly three years of full coverage for the estimated 46 million people in the United States who don't have health insurance. A million seconds from now you'll be a little over 11 days older. A billion seconds from now, you'll be 32 years older. A trillion seconds from now you and I will both be dust — that's 32,000 years into the future.

Now that the magnitude of what we're talking about here is a little bit more relatable, let's continue this brief survey of our current situation. I began studying the work of Robert Prechter back in 1986, met him in person the following year, and then saw him predict the 1987 crash just three days before it happened. Now he's saying that the last time the stock market looked the way it does today was just before that crash in 1987. As I've shared with my VRA subscribers before, his forecast for the Dow is 400. That's not a typo. Prechter predicts that when the Dow hits what he believes to be its true market bottom, it's going to correct all the way down to 400. I don't share his views entirely, but I do think the floor on the Dow may be as low as 2000 to 3000. Either way, it's bad news for anyone — individuals or institutions — whose financial survival depends on the health of the stock market. On his comparison between 1987 market conditions and the ones we're witnessing today I happen to agree with him completely.

While the word "recovery" keeps making strange and unsupported appearances in the main stream media, hardly anyone is talking about the re-emergence of the crisis in Europe. Ireland is in big, big trouble, Greece never left being in big trouble and Portugal is next. Spanish banks can't access the debt markets and the $1 trillion bailout of the European Union is in doubt.

Should the bailout be officially cancelled or radically modified or enlarged, all hell is going to break lose globally. All of this is happening in the face of big issues in China, where sources tell me that they have 60 million vacant homes that were built and never occupied. Their housing and commercial real estate crisis lies directly ahead, regardless of what you hear from the main stream media. Add to this the recognition that the US never really left our recession, which will soon be recognized as a Depression. At least that's what I call 17% unemployment based on the U-6 figure – the only one that matters. The U-6 figure includes those that are working part time because they cannot find a full time job, along with those that have been out of work for more than a year.

Finally, the bulls continue to say that "all is fine because corporate earnings have been strong." But they forget two very important things. First, the earnings numbers are phony to begin with because you just can't count the trillions in taxpayer-funded government stimulus payments as anything remotely close to real earnings. Second, bear markets like the one we're in now do not bottom out until the average price to earnings (P/E) multiple for the US stock market is in the 5-10 range. Since the recent P/E has been around 20, you can see realistically how much further we still have to fall. This is not the time to be invested in the stock market. This is the time to be short the stock market.

My long-time VRA subscribers know that I have spent the last 25 years or so developing a personal master-mind group with top financial gurus. Like Henry Ford, I know my personal limitations and the things that I can and cannot master, which meant that in order for me to discern the future of the markets and investing, I needed to find and develop relationships with the world's best and brightest. One of these gurus is Porter Stansberry, and while he writes for a competing investment newsletter, his work is among the best, specifically when it comes to forensic accounting. He sniffed out the General Motors fraud in 2005, and is now forecasting the same result for the US dollar and government debt along with all of the world's other fiat currencies. Stansberry points out that historically, not a single kind of paper money (fiat currency not backed by gold or other lasting stores of wealth) has ever survived. Another way he puts it is that gold remains undefeated in all of recorded history. There's no reason not to expect this trend to continue. Stansberry goes on to say that he can't recall any country that ever paid back its debts in real money once they'd reached 100% of GDP. All you have to do is look at the numbers.

There's only one way all of this can end. Before a bottom is in place we'll see the collapse of the Euro and continued destruction in the value of the US dollar, massive devaluation in stock prices in the range of 50-80%, and the completion of the deleveraging process that began in 2007/2008. The end result will be the worldwide recognition that the only true currency is gold and silver, but especially gold because the industrial uses of silver may have a dampening effect on its long-term upside (but possibly only somewhat). And with this will come the realization that the Federal Reserve (like all other central banks around the world) is nothing more than a criminal cartel, much like we perceive organized crime today. Can you imagine what the US political system will look like when this comes to pass? I'm guessing a complete return to the true spirit and intent of the Constitution is in order, along with the election of fiscal conservatives like my good friend Wayne Allyn Root and Ron Paul to the highest offices in the land. Maybe it will take calamity to restore common sense and honesty.

As we enter the most perilous financial times of the past 70 years, everyone is looking for answers. "Who is to blame for this? How bad will it get? What should I do now? Does the government really know what they're doing?" Instinctively, we all knew this house of cards would come crashing down at some point. However, as Napoleon Hill clearly established in the classic *Think and Grow Rich*, it's also possible to see the seeds of opportunity that come with every calamity. For the informed few who have prepared for the crisis – the smart money – they know that times like these are exactly when huge fortunes are made. Generational fortunes. The coming years will bring great values in real estate and stock markets, and as the cycles of history prove, these are the times when lasting legacies are created. Those who have armed themselves with new paradigm knowledge and put the right protective measures in place will be at the front of the line to take advantage of them.

CHAPTER THREE
HISTORY?
MORE LIKE "HISTORICAL FICTION"

Okay, maybe history doesn't really always repeat itself, as the old saying goes, but there's no question that it definitely rhymes. No two situations will ever be completely alike in every detail because the circumstances and people involved are always changing. But human nature seems to remain constant, and except for unpredictable natural disasters, most events tend to follow recognizable patterns and cycles once they're set in motion by human desires and motives, and sadly, sometimes by human weakness when we fail to live up to the best in ourselves. The economic turmoil we're seeing at home and around the world today bears a chilling resemblance to the dark chain of events that led up to the Great Depression. It's a fascinating story that reads like an industrial espionage thriller. The really fascinating part is that what actually happened has nothing to do with the "historical" fairy tales we've been fed by the cabal of career bureaucrats and the banking cartels.

They didn't call them the Roaring Twenties because money wasn't flowing freely or because consumers weren't spending it like there was no tomorrow. The newly created Federal Reserve System (1913) expanded credit by setting below-market interest rates and low reserve requirements that favored the big Wall Street banks. The Federal Reserve increased the money supply by 60% after the recession of 1921. By the end of the decade, "buying on margin" entered the American vocabulary as more and more investors overextended themselves to start speculating on a soaring stock market. This was partly because the 1920s also marked the beginning of capital-hungry mass production and gave rise to a culture of consumerism in America.

If you're looking for a symbol of American consumerism, you couldn't ask for a much more powerful one than the automobile. In 1919, there were just 6.7 million cars on American roads. By 1929, their number had exploded to more than 27 million – virtually one car for every household in the country. During this same period, banks offered the country's first home mortgages, and manufacturers of everything – from cars to everyday household items – allowed consumers to "buy on time." Installment credit skyrocketed during the 1920s. Statistics show that roughly 60% of all furniture and 75% of all radios – still the most ubiquitous form of home entertainment at the time – were bought on installment plans. Almost overnight, it seems, thrift and saving were replaced in the new consumer society by rampant spending and borrowing. Is any of this starting to sound familiar yet? Just wait. There's more.

Encouraging all this spending, the three Republican administrations of the 1920s practiced a kind of laissez-faire economics, beginning by chopping the top tax rates from 77% to 25% by 1925. Non-intervention into business and banking quietly became government policy. These policies led to a booming economy, and had it not been for the Fed's tampering, which led to overconfidence on the part of investors, followed by a classic credit-induced speculative boom, an orderly and strong economy would have continued. Instead, gambling in the markets by the banks and the wealthy increased. While the rich got richer, millions of Americans lived below the household poverty line of $2,000 per year. The days of wine and roses came to an abrupt end in October, 1929 with the Great Stock Market Crash.

Between 1929 and 1932, the market plummeted 89% from its high point. The cover story promoted by devotees of economist John Maynard Keynes (referred to by economics wonks as "Keynesians") is that Herbert Hoover's administration did nothing to try to bring the sputtering economy back to life. They say it took Franklin Delano Roosevelt and his Keynesian New Deal policies to save the country. It's a convincing story, except for the fact that it happens to be completely false. We'll explore this more deeply in a moment, but for now, just hold on to the idea that between 1929 and 1933, when Roosevelt came to power, the

Hoover administration actually increased real per-capita federal expenditures by 88% – not exactly what a sane observer would call an austerity program.

Most people know that the Great Depression officially lasted from 1929 until 1940. What is *not* well known is that the GDP was at the same level in 1936 where it had been in 1929. This was due in no small part to the fact that the GDP soared by 37% between 1933 and 1936. The unemployment rate in 1929 was 5%. In 1936, even after the GDP had recovered to pre-depression levels, the unemployment rate was still 15%. It spiked back to 18% in 1938 and stayed above 15% until World War II. It's significant to note that in 1936, private domestic investment was 21% below where it was back in 1929. In contrast to all of this, government expenditures surged by 46% between 1929 and 1936. While the government was busy creating an alphabet soup of expensive new agencies and hiring masses of people for make-work projects, private industry was being crowded out. Again, sound familiar? The extensive governmental economic intervention that began during the Hoover administration was expanded dramatically under FDR. The manipulation of wage rates and prices, expansion of credit, propping up of weak firms, and increased government spending on public works actually *prolonged* the Great Depression.

All of this evidence strongly contradicts the so-called "official" story promoted by Keynesians that the supposed 1937-38 Depression within the Great Depression was caused by Roosevelt becoming a believer in austerity. In fact, the GDP only dropped by 3.5% in 1938 and rebounded by 8.1% in 1939. What *actually* collapsed in 1938 was private investment, which fell 34%. By contrast, government expenditures declined by only 4.5% in 1938, confirming that Roosevelt did nothing to slash spending. If he took his foot off the gas pedal at all, it was by cutting back on jobs programs like those provided by the Works Progress Administration and the Public Works Administration.

And the reason for the private investment collapse? It was Roosevelt's vigorous new anti-business crusade. FDR denounced big business as the cause of the depression. In March 1938, Roosevelt appointed Yale University law professor Thurman Arnold to head up the antitrust division of the Justice Department. Arnold soon hired an army of 300 lawyers to file mountains of antitrust lawsuits against businesses. In some cases, Arnold waged legal war on entire industries, with lawsuits against milk, oil, tobacco, shoe machinery, tires, fertilizer, railroads, pharmaceuticals, school supplies, billboards, fire insurance, liquor, typewriters and movies.

The main stream media's popular narratives about the causes and cure for the Great Depression invariably start with the Beverly Hillbillies-style folksong we've all heard that the stock market crash caused the Great Depression. You can almost hear the banjoes in the next verse, where Herbert Hoover purportedly refused to spend government money in an effort to reinvigorate the economy. Roosevelt's New Deal government spending programs allegedly saved America. This folksong is another big lie. The

Great Depression was caused by Federal Reserve expansion of the money supply in the 1920s that led to an unsustainable credit-driven boom. Very familiar.

When the Federal Reserve finally started (or feigned?) belt-tightening in 1928, it was already too late to avoid financial collapse. According to Murray Rothbard, in his book *America's Great Depression*, the artificial interference in the economy was already a disaster *before* the depression, and government efforts to prop up the economy after the crash of 1929 only made things worse. If you want to read another great book on this period, I also recommend *FDR's Folly* by Jim Powell. Let's revisit Rothbard's point one more time for emphasis, because it has everything to do with why all this history should matter to you and me today. Here it is – government intervention during the Great Depression actually *delayed* the market's adjustment and made the road to complete recovery even more difficult.

Adding weight to this viewpoint is the work of Ludwig von Mises, another noted depression-era economics expert who was a proponent of what became known as the Austrian School. More on that in a later chapter. His theories about the behavior of free markets are behind some of today's most trustworthy voices of reason in economics and often ran in direct opposition to the ideas of John Maynard Keynes. Further proving that everything's connected, it's significant that Keynes was also a key player in the 1919 Versailles Treaty negotiations, sowing the seeds of the economic collapse that enabled Hitler's rise to power, and establishing the present day borders of Iraq – where over a trillion of your tax dollars have been spent.

You won't hear the likes of Greenspan, Bernanke, Paulson or Geithner quoting Ludwig von Mises (at least, not in a positive light), but it turns out that he had some very insightful remarks to make about what happened in the 1920s and 1930s. *"There is no means of avoiding the final collapse of a boom brought on by credit and fiat monetary expansion,"* he said. *"The only question is whether the crisis should come sooner in the form of a recession or later as a final and total catastrophe of depression as the currency systems crumble."* Von Mises' explanation accurately describes our present economic situation in America as confirmed by current headlines.

Digging deeper, some fascinating similarities with today's economy leap out when you examine the Bureau of Economic Analysis chart of Gross Domestic Product from 1929 to 1939. In 1929, consumer expenditures accounted for 72.3% of GDP, confirming that the American brand of borrow-and-spend consumerism we've heard so much about is not really a modern development at all. In fact, consumer spending peaked at 81% of GDP back in 1932 and remained above 70% throughout the entire depression. By 1950 consumer expenditures had subsided to 64% of GDP. In 1960, they had fallen to 63% and edged up to 64% by 1970, where they remained until 1980. By 1990 they had ticked up to 66% and by 2000 had reached 68%.

Many thought we had reached the modern-day climax in 2007 at 70% of GDP. However, in a replay of FDR's New Deal playbook, where much of the consumerism was funded by make-work projects and federal transfer payments, the federal government has thrown billions of dollars at consumers to buy houses, cars, and appliances. Consumer expenditures as a percentage of GDP actually rose to 71% in 2009. It should be readily apparent that until consumer expenditures are narrowed to a level that leads to a sustainable, balanced economy, the current depression will continue indefinitely.

The historic parallels with modern times are nothing less than uncanny. Not so long ago, former FED Chairman Alan Greenspan expanded the money supply right after the dot-com bust, dropped interest rates to 1%, encouraged a credit-driven boom, and created a gigantic housing bubble. By the time the FED acknowledged they had created a bubble, it was already too late. The government response to the 2008 financial collapse has been to once again expand the money supply, reduce interest rates to 0%, borrow and spend as much as $850 billion (and climbing) through the government's stimulus program - useless make-work pork projects, consumer spending programs for cars and appliances, and unevenly applied, incredibly ineffective tax credits and anti-foreclosure programs to artificially prop up housing. The national debt has been driven ever higher in recent months, with many trillions more in government guarantees along with trillions in Quantitative Easing, or QE, by the FED. I'll cover QE in more detail later, as it will be the fuse that lights the fire for the coming hyperinflation.

Now, are you ready to see how far down this rabbit hole really goes? Porter Stansberry, whose work I referenced earlier, is another one of those few "voices of reason" you can trust to provide truthful counterpoint to the historical fiction found in the main stream media and statements by other "experts" in our government agencies and financial institutions. In case you don't recognize his name, he's the one who took so much heat for his 2005 prediction that General Motors was headed for bankruptcy – until everyone found out he was right, simply because he took the courageously contrarian approach of looking honestly at the numbers. We can't quote whole passages here, but I encourage you to look them up because in his publications, Stansberry puts a number of chilling historical facts into perspective that go back even further than the Great Depression. He makes a convincing argument, along with mine, that the US is not only on its way to massive inflation, but that we've already passed the point where it's no longer avoidable. Since you've already gone back in time with me this far, maybe you're willing to go back just a little bit further.

It so happens that America isn't the first world power to default by way of inflation. In 1915, just after World War I got underway, one gold-backed US dollar would get you 4.2 German marks. Faced with the prospect of starvation and annihilation when they lost the war, Germany accepted armistice terms that required $12.5 billion in reparations. During the Versailles Treaty negotiations, John Maynard Keynes ruffled feathers with his prediction that $10 billion would be the most they could recover, but his figure turned out to be much more on target than the $300 billion his colleagues were pushing for. As it was, the debt they finally settled on was equal to 100% of Germany's pre-war GDP, but by this time the exchange rate had fallen to 65 marks to the dollar, a devaluation of about 95%. Here's where it starts to get interesting.

Folks have been led to believe that the hyperinflation to follow was caused by Germany's war debt, but that's not exactly what happened. After the war, Germany *was* stony broke, yes – but the mark was cheap and, to a lot of people, it looked like a great bargain basement investment opportunity. Gambling that Germany would somehow figure out how to refinance its debts down the road, speculators poured $2 billion of additional credit into the German economy. What could possibly go wrong? Several things, actually. First, although they'd live to regret it in a few short years, France pulled rank as Germany's biggest creditor and denied appeals to renegotiate the armistice terms. Next, the German population lost confidence in their own government and started protesting the war debts. That's when things started to get really ugly. In 1922, German consumers saw prices shoot up by a multiple of forty. Imagine what it would do to your household budget if you had to pay $400 for necessities that used to cost you $10. The mark continued its free fall from 190 down to 7,600 to the dollar. It was somewhere around this point that the assassinations started.

When Germany skipped a 1923 foreign debt payment, France and Belgium sent 40,000 troops in to collect. And you thought you had problems with collection notices you may have received on your past due obligations. Naturally, the German government responded by printing even more money. 17 trillion marks rolled off the government presses in 1923, compared with 1 trillion the year before. As a result, the exchange rate plummeted to 620,000 marks to the dollar by August of 1923 and by early November it was 630 billion to one.

Here's the significance of all this background. While it's not likely that Chinese troops will ever march into America to force repayment on our current debt obligations, what could happen instead is a lot worse than what they experienced in Weimar Germany. Why? For starters, unlike the US dollar, the mark was not the cornerstone of the world economy. As it stands today, over 60% of the world's bank reserves are US Treasury obligations. As the Fed continues to print more and more baseless fiat currency, the world's money supply continues to expand. Sooner or later, people are going to lose confidence in the stability of the exchange value of *any* kind of paper money, not just the US dollar. The massive inflation that follows won't just cripple the US economy, but will impact the entire world. Everything's connected.

I didn't walk you through all of this to bore you with an abstract history lesson. The most important insight to pick up here is that just like their predecessors, our politicians and monetary authorities have once again drawn the wrong conclusions from the lessons of the Great Depression. Referring back to the Gerald Celente insight I quoted earlier, we can learn to recognize where we're going by understanding where we've been. The result of all this will be a second, Greater Depression and more pain for an already overburdened and disappearing middle class. The investment consequences of these misguided government stimulus programs will be the further debasement of the currency and ultimately severe hyperinflation and surging interest rates.

Owning precious metals and mining stocks (value investments in true stores of wealth rather than in doomed fiat currencies), and shorting US Treasuries are some of the most powerful ways to protect yourself from these frightening and inevitable outcomes over the next few years. No matter what happens, it's impossible for me to overstate the importance of learning to think critically for yourself so that you can separate historical fact from historical fiction. *Crashproof Prosperity* means taking responsibility for your own financial education. I implore you to read, watch and listen with purpose so that you will be on the winning side as wealth changes hands from the ill-informed to the well-informed — *the old paradigm versus the new paradigm.* Which group are you in?

CHAPTER FOUR
THE INVISIBLE HAND

It's not the name of a horror film, but the story – all true – is orders of magnitude more frightening. I'm talking about *The Creature from Jekyll Island*, now in its fifth updated edition, by noted scholar, researcher and documentary filmmaker, as well as dear friend, G. Edward Griffin. It's a thick book and, between the sensational passages about the real historical figures involved, not exactly "light reading" due to Griffin's meticulous notes and supporting documentation. But it's an absolute must-read for anyone who wants to know the whole, true story behind the modern central banking system and how it directly impacts our lives.

The "creature" Griffin refers to in his book title is the secretive creation known as the Federal Reserve System, and Jekyll Island is a real place on the coast of Georgia, roughly halfway between Savannah to the north and Jacksonville, Florida to the south.

You may not believe in time travel, but once you read Griffin's important book, you'll know beyond a doubt that your pocket is literally being picked at this very moment (along with those of your parents and your grandparents and generations to come) by a small group of the world's most powerful bankers and influence peddlers, who met behind closed doors at a luxurious private coastal retreat nearly 100 years ago – 1910 to be exact.

The first thing you should know about the "Federal Reserve" is that it is not now, nor has it *ever* been a part of the government of the United States. It is privately owned and, due to the ingenuity and stealth of its creators, is in no way officially accountable to any real government authority. As a result, it's just as "federal" as Federal Express, although dramatically less reliable. And while we're on the topic of misnomers, you should also know that the Federal Reserve System has no real reserves, and in fact, is responsible for the recklessly loose fractional reserve lending standards that have made the collapse of our banking, currency and credit systems virtually inevitable. And of course we have the FED to thank for the US dollar's 95% collapse in value since the Federal Reserve Act was passed in1913. This "currency inflation" is destroying our middle class, yet none of this well-researched truth is taught in our schools or universities. Makes you wonder just a bit, doesn't it? The FED is not Federal and there are no Reserves! Classes with this exact title should be taught throughout the country – and around the world wherever a central bank like the FED exists (the Bank of Japan, and the European Central Bank to name just two) – because they're all sister organizations to the US FED.

We don't have time or space to go into all the history here, so I strongly encourage you to read *The Creature from Jekyll Island* for yourself to get the whole story. Griffin points out that many crucial conflicts between our nation's founding fathers (largely forgotten or ignored by today's talking heads) had to do with the insidious, unchecked power of central banks to undermine our constitutional freedoms and protections. As you can easily discover for yourself, it's clearly documented that powerful outside interests made numerous overt and covert attempts to allow central banking to infiltrate the United States, against the protests of those who knew better. The founders who had their hearts and minds in the right place issued wise and stern warnings not only to their peers, but also to future generations, to protect themselves at all costs from the corrosive dangers of the European central banking abuses they'd just escaped by way of the Revolutionary War. The visionary Thomas Jefferson said it best; *"I believe that banking institutions are more dangerous to our liberties than standing armies. If the American people ever allow private banks to control the issue of their currency, first by inflation, then by deflation, the banks and corporations that will grow up around [the banks] will deprive the people of all property until their children wake-up homeless on the continent their fathers conquered. The issuing power should be taken from the banks and restored to the people, to whom it properly belongs."*

Sadly, in spite of all the protective measures the founding fathers tried to put in place, the persistent uber-bankers eventually won, due in no small part to the clever naming trick they invented. In his wonderful inspirational talks, even a positive guy like Zig

Ziglar points out how a very subtle difference in the way you word something can have a huge influence on the outcome. *"If you tell your wife she's a vision, it means something completely different than if you tell her she's a sight."* Which government initiative would you be more likely to support — socialized medicine, or the public plan? An arms-for-hostages swap or good will gifts to freedom fighters? Mission accomplished or an endless and deadly Middle Eastern money pit? Virtually unlimited power for the executive branch to suspend any citizen's constitutional protections or a "Patriot Act" (that your elected representatives never had time to read)?

Although he didn't actually word it this succinctly, the official marketing policy of Adolph Hitler's National Socialist Worker's Party was in essence that *"...the bigger the lie, the more people will believe it."* The bankers at the secret Jekyll Island gathering, unquestionably among the world's most intelligent and successful businessmen in their day, also knew this. What better way to disguise a privately controlled enterprise designed to circumvent economic checks and balances than to name it after (and thereby neutralize) your most dangerous opponent — the institutions representing the American people? When the powerbrokers behind the largest private banks got word through their moles and toadies that tough legislation was about to be passed to restrict their powers, they graciously volunteered to draft the language themselves, in secret, which was then hand-carried through the halls of congress and quietly adopted as the law of the land. That's what happened at Jekyll Island and that's why, to this day, the FED — the all-powerful private central bank our founding fathers tried to avoid — has *never* been audited. What's in a name? Everything.

Fortunately for all of us, G. Edward Griffin is not the only voice of reason out there. Believe it or not, there are a handful of economists, statesmen, reporters and statisticians with the courage and integrity to do their own due diligence, rather than just blindly accepting stories from the fox that's watching the henhouse. I mention several of them in *Crashproof Prosperity* and you'll see me quote them often in my VRA updates. I invite you to seek them out for yourself, evaluate the information on its own merits and form your own opinions. My business partner and Wealth Masters Co-Founder, Karl Bessey posted the following appeal to audit the Federal Reserve on his highly popular blog. Since I could not have worded it better, and with full credit to Karl, I'm going to quote for you here the eloquent case he makes that it's past time to not only *open* the books, but to *close* the Fed and shut it down once and for all.

"I started this blog with the intention of keeping politics out of it. But I'm having a hard time doing that these days with all the B.S. that is going on in Washington. For those of you that know me, you know that freedom and liberty are passions of mine. Through my lifetime, I have witnessed our civil liberties being taken away one at a time. Where will we be in another generation if things continue on this path? I 'm sitting here in amazement as our lawmakers in Washington spend our country into oblivion with no end in sight.

It's the Federal Reserve System that makes this reckless spending possible and keeps us all in debt. More spending is not going to fix the problem, but will simply put off the inevitable that will happen in the near future when it all comes crashing down. Mark my words on this. If you think the current administration's plans are going to work, you are living in la-la land. Our government can't run Amtrak, the Postal Service, Fannie Mae, Freddie Mac, and next they want to take over health care? You have to be joking!

I can go on and on, but the reason for my post today is to ask for your help to pass House Bill 2511. This is the bill introduced by Congressman Ron Paul from Texas (the last true statesman in Washington), and now has 282 cosponsors. I am proud to say that my representatives in Utah, both Congressmen and Senators, are also backing this bill. This will finally, after almost 100 years of the FED, let us see the books. The Chairman of the Federal Reserve, Ben Bernanke, was recently asked to go before a hearing to find out where all the money has gone, and he simply said 'no thanks.' It is time to get some answers. We have been under the rule of the Federal Reserve for far too long and it's time to let the masses know exactly how the FED operates. This could be the first nail in the coffin for the FED. Let's hope so. Remember that as evil as the FED already was on its own, the current administration in Washington actually wants to give it even more power. Don't let this happen. Pink Floyd is one of my favorite Rock Bands of all time. They have a song that states, "...united we stand, divided we fall." Those words could not ring more true in these times. Now is the time for each of us to rise up and let our elected officials know that it's time to get the job done."

Karl mentioned our current Federal Reserve Chairman, Ben Bernanke, who frequently testi-lies before congress about the US and global economies. For those that have followed my work in the past, you might recall how much fun I have catching Bernanke (and Greenspan before him) in one massive lie after another. Let me put it this way, if Bernocchio (Pinocchio plus Bernanke) were my son, he and his ever-growing nose would be grounded for life. I'd also have him stand in the corner — long nose against the wall — until he learned the importance of speaking the truth. Bernocchio's real parents must be ashamed. Where's Geppetto when you really need him?

Bernocchio's quotes do a much better job than I could ever do to underscore the flawed reasoning and outright falsehoods behind the rhetoric we routinely hear from the Federal Reserve and how disconnected they seem to be from reality. Here are just a few of my favorites.

June, 2010: *"The private sector is beginning to take over this recovery, and the US economy is now on a sustainable track. The economy ... appears to be on track to continue to expand through this year and next."* (Congressional testimony)

March, 2007: *"The impact on the broader economy and financial markets of the problems in the subprime market seems likely to be contained."* (The Economic Outlook: Joint Economic Committee, U. Congress)

February, 2008: *"I expect there will be some failures. I don't anticipate any serious problems of that sort among the large internationally active banks that make up a very substantial part of our banking system."* (The Guardian)

June, 2008: *"Despite a recent spike in the nation's unemployment rate, the danger that the economy has fallen into a 'substantial downturn' appears to have waned"* (MSNBC)

July, 2008: (Stated just two months before they needed over $100 billion in taxpayer bailouts) *"...no danger of failing... adequately capitalized"* (In reference to Freddie Mac and Fannie Mae on CBS)

And this man is considered by many to be the second most powerful individual on the planet? The professor that has it all figured out and that will save us from economic Armageddon? The reality is that Bernocchio cannot, and should not be trusted. By simply doing the opposite of what he recommends you could have made a fortune over the years, and the same held true with his predecessor, Mr. Greenspan. Sounds like a good game plan going forward.

Maybe it's just that they have trouble getting it right when the press puts them on the spot. Let's see how they do when stage fright isn't a factor and they have time to get their thoughts together in a written statement, when they're away from the pressure of all those cameras and lights. Here's a response from the Federal Reserve to a letter they received asking whether or not they manipulate the stock markets. As my VRA readers know, this issue is more than just something that I *suspect* is happening – it *has* been happening for many years. All of the evidence proves to me that this is *exactly* what they're doing. In fairness, I'll let the FED go first. Here's the key line from their reply: *"I want to assure you that the Federal Reserve's monetary policy actions are not aimed at correcting or influencing any particular market."*

When I first read this, I couldn't believe my eyes. Their actions are not aimed at influencing *any* market? Let's see. On a daily basis the FED forces the US Treasury to print tens of billions in new US dollars, which the FED acquires for virtually nothing and then disperses into the markets as they see fit. The end result? Massive currency inflation! This is a fact, and no one would dare dispute it. And how about *this* for manipulation? The FED uses much of this free money to purchase trillions of our own debt! The FED routinely buys US Treasury bonds, mortgage-backed securities, and essentially any toxic debt instrument they deem necessary to keep this near worthless debt from flooding the markets. This is another fact that no one disputes. Heck, the FED even announces these transactions when they take place (or at least some of them) through Quantitative Easing (currently on QEII) and POMO (Permanent Open Market Operations).

These exact actions have been used to remove a huge supply of overhanging debt from our supposedly free market economy, which in turn forces down interest rates. The FED's view is that lower interest rates stimulate borrowing and cause investors to take more risk with their investment dollars in hopes of a better return. And somehow we're supposed to believe this statement that their actions are not aimed at influencing the markets? And of course they never actually denied that they buy stocks. Their non-denial is an admittance of guilt. And yes, by the way, the European Central Bank and Bank of Japan – in fact all central banks – do the same things routinely.

To be completely fair about this, actions really do speak louder than words. Maybe all those brainy economists at the FED are just numbers guys and really aren't that gifted verbally. After all, they're hired for the *results* they get, not what they *say*, right? Let's take a look at some of the policies they've implemented and see if they ring true in action more than they do in their public statements. Just for fun, let's start with Quantitative Easing (QE). These two words had no real meaning or significance, at least not in the main stream media, until the crash of 2008 really got going. That's when the Federal Reserve decided to begin playing God with the US and global economies to an even greater extent than they had before. All they did in the "old days" was debase the currency by printing it into oblivion. The result was massive currency inflation and a 95% drop in purchasing power – the reason that in most families both spouses have to work – the direct result being the destruction of the middle class, which is nearing its final stages globally.

After the Lehman Brothers collapse in September 2008, it was a whole new ballgame. The US government, the Federal Reserve (and all of the central banks and their participating governments globally) decided to do something that even they had never done before. Led by the FED, they all decided to begin buying up their *own* debt. It's pretty simple, really – the Treasury Department issues bonds to raise money, and then the Federal Reserve is *the* buyer. So far the FED has purchased well over $2 trillion in US government debt and toxic mortgage debt, making the Federal Reserve the largest holder of US debt in the world, surpassing even China. Incredibly 90% of this happened in less than 18 months, where China took well over a decade to accumulate most of their US debt holdings.

This is what the FED calls Quantitative Easing and it's leading to the complete demise of our economic system as we know it. It's a sign of admitted desperation and has the Obama administration's fingerprints all over it because we already know how desperate they are to breathe signs of life into the economy. A rumor hit the Street back in October of last year that the FED was about to launch QEII (no, not the cruise ship, but a not-so-slow boat to financial ruin), and in fact this was announced on November 3. This time they will likely double their purchases of US debt and continue to expand the program to include not just Treasury bonds, but additional toxic debt as well. This includes *all* of the commercial and residential housing debt that's clogging up the balance sheets of our bankrupt banks, thanks in large part to the government's March, 2009 decision to allow banks to forego mark to market accounting, the accepted accounting principal for ages.

This cements the fact that they're repeating *every* mistake that Japan has made over the last 20+ years – mistakes that led to a more than 80% drop in their stock market and created a zombie economy for over two decades, resulting in falling real estate prices each and every year. And while action in the stock market may look positive in the short term (like throwing fuel on a dying fire) this sugar high is an incredibly destructive move that guarantees a future of massive hyperinflation. As success expert Stephen Covey likes to say, *"...you're free to choose your actions, but you're not free to choose the consequences...you can't pick up one end of a stick without picking up the other."* This is why I have warned for years about the coming unintended consequences.

The FED's actions are rife with unintended consequences, and as I've already emphasized several times in these pages, everything's connected. Yes, massive liquidity injection into the economy is just what Wall Street loves, so it's natural to see a brief uptick as a "positive" outcome of one FED action or another. But remember these two words and note them well – *unintended consequences*. Once the world realizes that this Frankenstein-like experiment with monetary policy can only result in bigger and deeper losses on our debt (while doing nothing at all to reverse 17% real unemployment), that's when the real global panic will set in. Could this massive level of money and debt creation buy them more time, and lead to a stock market rally in the short-term? Sure, anything's possible.

Let's take a closer look at that idea. Does the FED's manipulation give the market temporary buying signals from time to time? Sure it does. Yet, at the same time we continue to see daily economic announcements reminiscent of the Great Depression era. Unemployment is getting worse by the day, housing is still in the dumps and set for its next big leg down, and the poverty rate is at a generational low. This reminds me almost exactly of the summer of 2008 when the Dow Jones rose from under 11,000 to almost 12,000 less than one month before the Lehman Brothers bankruptcy. The trading looks identical – a bear market rally on exceedingly light volume with massive amounts of insider selling. Does this really feel like a bull market to you, or to anyone you know that's still trying to make ends meet?

In late 2008, after the Lehman bankruptcy and near implosion of the global financial system, Treasury Secretary Henry Paulson was quoted as saying to top people in government, *"This is war gentlemen. The complete collapse of our financial way of life is at stake."* He was right – this *is* war. And we know that in war, all strategies are on the table. Following the crash of 1987, or Black Monday, as it came to be known, I watched the powers that be at the FED and Treasury form the highly secretive group known as the PPT, or Plunge Protection Team. Everyone on the Street referred to it as the invisible hand, because while you couldn't see it, you could certainly feel it in action. The PPT was purportedly formed to place a floor under the market during stock market panics to avoid another one-day crash like the ones that happened in 1929 and 1987. To me, the creation of the "invisible hand" marked the beginning of the end of our free market system, and it's very much alive and operating on steroids today.

Alan Greenspan, among others, has all but admitted the existence of the PPT, and it's now common knowledge that these "masters of the universe" reside in real life at 33 Liberty Street, the current home of the Federal Reserve Bank of New York in downtown Manhattan. And because the FED has access to unlimited amounts of newly printed US dollars (again, recall the fact that they have *never* been audited), there's literally nothing that they cannot do – least in their overinflated and delusional sense of right and wrong. This situation is nothing short of a criminal conflict of interest, and yes, it *is* war.

Here's one important reason why these actions by the FED aren't sustainable. Over the next three years, over 60% of all US debt matures. The Obama administration has kept the vast amount of maturities in short term debt financing, which is just about all that China and our other foreign masters will agree to buy due to their concerns about our long term ability to make good on our promises to pay. This means that anywhere from $6 trillion to $8.5 trillion in American sovereign debt will mature over the next 36 months. In order keep the house of cards propped up, we must replace this maturing debt with new debt, not to mention the additional $1 trillion or more we have to issue every year to keep funding our bankrupt federal budget.

And this is just the tip of the iceberg when it comes to the emerging sovereign debt crisis. Japan is in even worse shape. With a debt to GDP ratio of 200% (outside of Zimbabwe the highest in the world), they're staring straight down the barrel of a requirement to replace as much as $2.5 trillion in debt over just the next 12 months. In the past, their aging baby boomers purchased most of it, but now that the boomers are reaching retirement age, they'll become spenders of that money, rather than savers. This situation is all the more serious because population growth in Japan is at its lowest in modern history. Where will the new earners and savers come from to keep feeding the system? And then of course there's the European Union and its colossally bankrupt system, which has to find buyers for over $1 trillion of maturing debt over the next year, with gobs more obligations coming right behind the ones they have now.

That's why "this is war" has become such an important concept when we take a closer look at the consequences of manipulation by the FED and their international counterparts. Global governments are beyond desperate to reignite the world economy. Collectively, they're all under pressure (and competition!) to find buyers for more than $10 trillion in increasingly risky new government debt over the next one to three years, and without these buyers, the crash of 2008 will look positively tame in comparison to what follows. As powerful as these "masters of the universe" may appear to be in the short term, they're no match for the financial laws of reality in the long term. This is the universal law that will determine the outcome of the economic war, rather than the short term battles being waged today.

For all of those in the main stream media that either can't read *real* history books (or simply choose to ignore them); the Great Depression would have continued well into the 1940s had WWII not intervened. As a direct result of the same approach we're taking now (massive government expansion), the *real* economy never had a chance to get going – the natural deleveraging process was not allowed to take place. This is a simplistic review of course, but now we have the Obama administration and very complicit Republicans leading us down the very same dead end road that was paved by FDR. These guys are desperate and nothing they do should surprise us. Remember, unemployment averaged 14% through the 1930s, and was on its way up again going into WWII (approximately 18% by 1938). It's precisely because of the widely mistaken view that FDR did a good job of getting us out of the Great Depression that Barack Obama and Ben Bernanke feel compelled to repeat the same disastrous mistakes. We all know what happened around the globe following (and because of) the Great Depression. We can only hope that the world does not begin to repeat those same horrors all over again, much less create another Adolph Hitler.

Here's the bottom line. A system built on phony money cannot possibly last. Unchecked financial manipulation – financial engineering – by the secretive Federal Reserve and their partners in crime around the world cannot last. There is no way this ends well, and this is why you must prepare now for the coming storm, just as common sense tells you to buy winter coats in the summer. These are the precise events and consequences I've been warning everyone about for years. Thanks to the reckless intervention of the FED, any chance we had of coming out of this recession (soon to be a depression) is now 20% at best. In this environment you'll see gold and silver rise at least another 300% in the next two to three years. This is why you must buy gold and silver and make other protective moves now, like avoiding government and municipal debt, and steering clear of personal debt, along with old paradigm investments in the stock market, such as mutual funds. When the light switch is turned off, the speed of the collapse will make preparation all but impossible. And those still trapped in the old paradigm mindset will be wiped out.

CHAPTER FIVE
BECAUSE I SAID SO

How far did you get protesting *that* one with your folks? About as far as you'll get with the Federal Reserve, I'm afraid, when you ask them why you should treat the fiat currency they print by the boxcar load as if it were real money. In oversimplified terms, "because I said so" is pretty much what the word "fiat" boils down to. No, I'm not talking about the car. Most dictionary definitions of fiat go something like this; *1. A command or act of will that creates something without or as if without further effort. 2. An authoritative determination. 3. An authoritative or arbitrary order.* The word comes down to us from the Latin expression for "let it be done." Our modern concepts of decrees, edicts, directives, rulings and even the authoritative Vatican documents called "Papal Bulls" can all be traced back to the same idea. By extension, the very next dictionary entry defines *fiat money* as money (paper currency) not convertible into coin or specie of equivalent value.

You see, a well documented but barely publicized global financial metamorphosis has been in play for a long time that forever changed the world as we know it. As a result, many of the things we've always taken for granted will no longer remain the same. For the first time ever, a fiat currency system is now in place in every country on the planet. Simply put, every financial system in the world is now based on currencies that have *nothing of value* backing them. In 1971, with the help of President Richard M. Nixon, the US was the last major industrialized nation to go off what was known as "the gold standard" where a country's basic unit of currency – the dollar in our case – is equal to (and exchangeable for) a specific amount of gold.

This "paper currency" system seemed to work for a while, but the financial implosion that started in 2008 sparked a systemic financial meltdown with ramifications we're only beginning to see. The result will be rampant hyperinflation, skyrocketing interest rates, and a global bear market in stocks. Curiously to most, this will also send other specific investments soaring in price.

In the years ahead, we'll all look back and see that when global governments shanghaied the world's economies, it was the beginning of the end for capitalism and a true free market system. President Obama and his handlers love to point to the American style of capitalism as the root cause of all the financial woes we're experiencing today. Now, I've heard some weak arguments in my time, but anyone with a little intellectual honesty and at least a minimal capacity for abstract thought knows the truth. Capitalism isn't to blame.

The failure lies with the Federal Reserve System's fiat currency and fractional reserve banking, the military-industrial complex and its imperialistic goals, fraudulent government entities like Fannie Mae and Freddie Mac, unions that have helped to drive tens of millions of high quality manufacturing jobs offshore, and the creation of more than $700 trillion in unregulated toxic derivatives. And finally, a big share of the credit goes to the corrupt and/or inept politicians and bankers who enabled $100 trillion in US debt that can never be paid off and the erosion of our buying power with paper dollars that perpetually decline in value with each new press run.

A decent rally in the US dollar did place a short-term cap on precious metals in 2009, but the rally quickly reversed course as investors around the world realized that no fiat currency on the planet is safe from the dangers of the printing press, especially the greenback. Again, once Nixon took the US off the gold standard in 1971, we officially joined every other country on the planet with a currency backed by nothing — nothing except the "full faith and credit" of that particular country. Now, with each passing day investors are asking themselves how much faith they have in the ability of their government to manage the economy with any degree of fiscal soundness.

The bottom line is that if you and I ran our household or business finances the way global governments run theirs, our banks and creditors would confiscate everything we owned in less than a week. The difference of course is that you and I can't print our own money. That's why they built Ft. Leavenworth. Mark my words; within the next three years – and likely sooner – our economy is headed for precisely that end result.

If you think that hyperinflation and a currency/debt default can't happen here, then you need to read a good history book where you'll find mind-boggling documentation of this very thing happening in Zimbabwe, Argentina, Russia and Germany, just to name a few. In the near future we'll be hearing about defaults and hyperinflation in Ireland, Greece, Spain, Italy and Portugal, followed by another wave of currency collapses in Hungary and Lithuania. Shortly thereafter you'll see it happen in Japan and the UK – just before it hops across the pond. By then, all the institutions we've looked to in the past for salvation and quick fixes will be powerless to stop it. If rescue measures have any effect at all, history has taught us the sobering truth that whatever "they" do will only worsen and prolong the inevitable.

Slowly and insidiously, we've all gotten used to the idea of inflation over the years. Consider this – since the Federal Reserve was created in 1913 the US dollar has lost 95% of its purchasing power. Because it happened gradually over a period of nearly a century, we barely noticed it from one year to the next. It's like boiling a frog. Throw one into a pot of hot water and he'll jump right out – but if you raise the temperature slowly, the frog won't notice until it's too late. We're in the early stages of massive hyperinflation now, except this time you and I are the frogs. In the beginning, the water feels fine and all looks good as the economy appears to recover. The stock market rises, green shoots seem to emerge, and consumer confidence starts to rebound a little. But don't be fooled. Before this is over, we'll be cursing the government, the FED, and every politician that voted for trillions in taxpayer funded bailouts and stimulus programs that resulted in the final destruction of our fiat currency.

In total, the US has more than $100 trillion in debt when you take all the real figures into account, namely entitlement programs like social [in]security, Medicare and Medicaid and our current $14 trillion government debt. That's $100,000,000,000,000 my friends, and if we return to those pallets of 100 dollar bills we talked about earlier, our hypothetical little person standing next to the money probably wouldn't even be visible anymore without a microscope. Like all debt, ours has interest attached to it that has to be paid, and obviously, the principal will eventually have to be repaid as well. Not long from now, when the world (China, Japan, the Middle East and other creditors) officially recognizes that we'll *never* be able to repay this ridiculous and historically unprecedented level of debt, interest rates *must* begin to rise. Can you feel the water getting hotter now?

Think about it this way. If you have a poor credit rating and need to borrow money from a bank to buy a home or car, it's your projected ability to repay the loan (the odds that you'll default based on your credit history) that the bank will use to determine your interest rate. Now, think of China and our other foreign creditors (masters) as the bank. Folks, it will be just like a light switch going off. One day, all will be fine and our bond market will appear stable, and the next day it *just won't*. Virtually without notice, interest rates will start to shoot up and the bond market's decline will suddenly pick up speed. You see, with real interest rates near zero, where they are today, the interest on $14 trillion – must less $100 trillion – may seem like no big deal. And this total does not even include the $2 trillion or so that our states need to fund their own bankrupt budgets, or the $3 trillion that's needed to fund a US pension system that's been robbing Peter to pay Paul for the last 10 years. But the ability to fund this mess is all going to change very quickly when foreign creditors get nervous and force us to choose between accepting increasing interest rates on their US investments or kissing them goodbye.

No one on CNBC will be able to explain exactly why things appear to be getting worse, but we'll all know the answer. Just like the late 1970s and early 1980s, we'll see a spike up in rates and inflation that will continue to feed on itself. The speed of change will be breathtaking to the unprepared, and those that wait too long to take action will feel like they're stuck in quicksand – they'll know they need to get out but there won't be much they can do about it. This is why it's so important to take action now. Make sure you're diversified *out* of the US dollar (all fiat currencies globally), stocks that will take a direct hit and into inflation-positive investments. I can't tell you exactly when rates will begin to rise sharply, only that they inevitably will, and that I believe it will be much sooner than later. Then, an already weak economy truly will become a depression.

Here's another crucial reason why "fiat currency" is a term you need to know and understand. I first recommended gold at just below $300/ounce in 2002/2003. Since then gold and silver have risen close to 400% and we've seen a 40 to 70 % gain in gold and silver in the past year alone. Key mining stocks, where the real money has been made, have seen gains of anywhere from 300% to 1500% in the two years, and now you're beginning to understand why. On top of this, every "real" financial guru I follow is buying precious metals aggressively and will continue to do so. We already knew that the Chinese have been buying precious metals aggressively for a couple of years, but now they've increased their buying to record levels and are allowing the Chinese population to do so as well. That's well over a billion people that can now buy precious metals. Gold is now a momentum trade like oil and will soon become *the* must-hold currency globally. It won't be long before you'll see gold start to spike several hundred dollars an ounce in a single day. And that, my friends, will signal the beginning of the end of our paper currency system – a currency backed by nothing and copied all over the world.

Right now you could be asking yourself, as any reasonable person might, why we don't just go ahead and put ourselves back on the gold standard again. Why not indeed? That same question may have been on the mind of Congressman Ron Paul (also from my great home state of Texas!) when he wondered out loud about the status of the legendary gold reserves in Fort Knox. Fox News picked up on the story immediately and ran with it big time. Not only is the Republican Congressman questioning whether there's any gold left at Fort Knox, he'd also like proof that the Federal Reserve owns any gold and is calling for an independent audit to verify that America's gold reserves are really as substantial as officials claim they are.

Ron Paul is gaining recognition for fiercely opposing anything connected to the Federal Reserve System and has been quoted as saying the public deserves to know what's really inside America's gold vaults — especially in the event that gold is ever reinstated as the basis for the US dollar. *"It'd be nice for the American people to know whether or not the gold is there,"* he said in a Fox Business Network interview. He went on to say that if it is all there, the citizens have a right know if any of it has been obligated. And now that the Tea Party has helped to change the make-up of Congress, Ron Paul will have some like-minded friends to help (including his son Rand, the new senator from Kentucky).

No visitors are allowed inside Kentucky's ultra-secure Fort Knox facility, where gold worth billions of dollars is reportedly hidden behind 750 tons of reinforced steel and thousands of cubic feet of concrete and granite. The mystique of the place, which made a farcical appearance in the James Bond thriller *Goldfinger*, is the stuff of legend on the scale of epic films like *National Treasure* or *The Da Vinci Code*. The US Mint, which includes Fort Knox, is subjected to regular audits and reports that gold is temporarily removed in "very small quantities" only for this purpose, and that no other gold has been moved in or out for a very long time. The latest audit, prepared by KPMG, apparently didn't detail any gold holdings but did report that gold and silver continue to be held at Fort Knox.

In an interview with Kitco News, Ron Paul said there's *"reason to be suspicious"* about US gold holdings and suggested that in the absence of public accountability, officials could conceivably manipulate the price of gold to prop up the perceived value of paper money. The Congressman said *"it is a possibility"* that neither Fort Knox nor the New York Federal Reserve vaults contain any gold at all. In the same interview, he also said that it's time for the US government to legalize the use of gold and silver as legal tender alongside the dollar. *"If people get tired of using the paper standard, they can deal in gold or silver."* So far, there's been no response from the Treasury Department or the US Mint on Paul's proposal. He's raised the concern that the government is setting the stage for a depression by trying to print, spend and regulate its way out of the recession. *"Who knows? Someday we might want to have a gold standard again and quit all this printing-press money,"* Paul said to Fox Business Network, *"so it would be nice to know how much we have."*

I'm writing this just as the mid-term election results are in, and we know that Republicans have regained the House, but not the Senate. With Democrats in control of both houses, any meaningful investigations like the one Ron Paul is calling for were virtually impossible. However, with Republicans back in control of the house, Representative Darrell Issa, the Republican who heads the House Committee for Oversight and Government Reform, will have full subpoena power. He's already stated publicly that he intends to use that power —aggressively — not to mention the fact that he's worth over $160 million, meaning that he's personally beholden to no one in the fiat currency cabal.

With this possibility in mind, put yourself in the shoes of Obama, Geithner and Bernanke. Just the idea of investigations like the one Ron Paul proposes must scare the-you-know-what out of them. That's another reason why I don't trust these three. With the threat of major investigations on the horizon, they have the means, motive and opportunity to do just about anything they want to retain power. "Anything" could include fudging economic data to make it look like the economy is doing better than it really is – or possibly giving the FED the secretive (and illegal) ability to buy stocks aggressively so that market value continues to shoot up. Call me cynical, but based on what I've seen from this administration, I'd be surprised if these aren't the exact conversations they're having.

Here's the reality check. Gold and silver are the only real currencies on the planet, and when the Federal Reserve is forced to kick the printing presses into high gear to fund our massive budget and interest payment shortfalls, the new highs for precious metals are going to shock 99.9% of the population. I've mentioned Porter Stansberry a couple times so far and here's his take on fiat currency. *"Years from now, children currently under the age of 4 will be shocked to learn that their parents once earned, saved and invested with paper money. By the time they are old enough to know what money is, the entire paper money system will have collapsed. Historians will wonder how we could have all fallen for such a major con."*

What's important to remember is that the US and other global governments have thrown trillions upon trillions in funny money into the global financial system, and with interest rates being held at artificially low levels, all of this fiat currency has to go somewhere. Can you guess where it's going? Into the most liquid investments around – government bonds and blue chip stocks. A while back I woke up to more negative earnings results on CNBC and it got me thinking back to my days as a financial advisor and venture capitalist. It's never been more difficult for the average person to invest in the stock market and don't look for that to change anytime soon.

People are waking up to the reality of this economic crisis and wondering if they should get out, buy more, or just keep their eyes closed, hold on and hope for the best. Trust me on this one folks; it's going to get ugly before it's all over. The average mutual fund investor is going to start freaking out when they see the market hit new lows, because the consensus is that the government finally has things under control. Quick question; have you ever known the government to have things under control? Speaking of Ron Paul, this is the perfect point to recommend his best seller *The Revolution.* If you've ever been tempted to believe that big government is the answer to our problems, then his book is another must-read for you, as is *Atlas Shrugged*, the all-time classic on "reasoned thought" written by Ayn Rand in 1957.

You see, you're making a choice right now whether you realize it or not. 99% of the population has no idea what's coming or how to prepare for it, much less how to prosper greatly from it. As the fiat currency scam enters its final days, I urge you to use the time you have left (before these cataclysmic events reach their climax) to make sure your choices are the right ones for yourself, for your family and for those you care deeply about. As Robert

74

Redford's character says in the espionage thriller movie *Spy Game, "...when did Noah build the Ark? Before it started raining!"* The answers are made clear to those that make a commitment to seek out the truth and take responsibility for their own financial education. Are you sick and tired of being taken in by scams like fiat currency? In spite of all the disinformation that's out there, it's still possible to get unbiased, conflict-free, integrity-based materials on financial literacy, like the ones you'll find inside of Wealth Masters International. The important thing is to find a source you can trust, stick to it diligently and then read, watch and listen with purpose.

CHAPTER SIX
A FINANCIAL FRANKENSTEIN

I've mentioned Wall Street's "masters of the universe" comparison a couple times already. The idea came from *Bonfire of the Vanities*, Tom Wolfe's searing novel about the New York financial scene. Wolfe's instant classic was published in 1987, and I read it shortly thereafter. Although his story is fictional, the Wall Street players he writes about are based on the real-life greed and corruption that drives many of the world's most powerful financial firms. Without question, the book is far more applicable today than when it was first written nearly a quarter century ago. Meanwhile, in today's world, our flesh and blood "masters of the universe" — with obscene bonuses to prove it — are being taken down one after another by their own idiotic inventions. As you can see from the chapter heading, the possible metaphors for their wacky experiments are so thick here that there's enough material to fill several seasons of satire on Comedy Central's entire schedule run, plus the late night lineups on all the major networks.

The problem is, nobody's laughing at the consequences, except maybe for a shadowy handful of the world's most powerful central banking masterminds, who always seem to find a last minute escape hatch as they profit from the human misery of enslavement to debt. Let's take a look at a few of these bizarre science projects from Wall Street's version of Frankenstein's laboratory and see how they went horribly wrong. Unintended consequences, remember? Oh, but don't worry – the mad scientists in this story are all going to be okay – the monsters they let loose are coming after you and me, not their creators.

The top five firms on Wall Street were thought to be "too big to fail." But now Bear Stearns is gone, Lehman Brothers is gone, Merrill was forced to sell out to Bank of America to avoid insolvency, and then the last big names, J.P. Morgan and Goldman, waved the white flag and petitioned the government to allow them to become ordinary deposit taking banks – amazing. By reaching into taxpayers' pockets for over $850 billion in bailout funds, the government continues to sustain insolvent, criminally run Wall Street banks and dreadfully run companies like Fannie Mae, Freddie Mac, AIG, Citibank, General Motors, and Chrysler. The corporate leaders who profit most from these taxpayer-funded golden parachutes are often minority owners in these failed companies with virtually none of their own skin in the game – and nothing to lose. The misguided "rescue" efforts to keep these "walking dead" or zombie institutions on artificial life support prolong the agony for all of us by not allowing the real economy to bottom out naturally and begin an authentic recovery based on sustainable fiscal policies.

Another consequence of all this inept and short-sighted "financial engineering" on Wall Street is that it adds several trillion dollars of phantom liquidity to the global economy. The end result is that it's becoming increasingly difficult for anyone to evaluate investment risks or rewards because of the system's built-in conflicts of interest and the devastating abuses of derivatives (more on that in the next chapter). Add to all of this the fact that the stock market has become a rigged, extremely over-valued insiders-only game, and we now have the very real probability for long term bear market that could be far worse than anything we've seen in this country since the 1930s.

Based on historical figures, the stock market (as measured by the earnings of companies that make up the S&P 500 and the Dow Jones) will need to fall by at least 50% just to return to a normal price to earnings (P/E) multiple. You see, bear markets of this magnitude (driven by a massive deleveraging process that at the end of the day must run its course) do not bottom until we have reached a P/E of about 7. With a current P/E of about 20, we still have a way to go before reaching a real bottom – and this assumes that earnings stay constant – something that I see as highly unlikely. The ripple effect this will have on both stock prices and the overall economy will be enormous, which is why informed (and contrarian) investment choices are so crucial for survival, let alone prosperity. Those who follow the markets know that we've already seen the stock market drop by about 50% (just as I predicted) in every major index since the onslaught of the crisis in 2008, and my current work tells me that the coming declines will surpass even the March 2009 lows – and by a large degree. Unfortunately, the next big leg down will be quick and painful for most. Ultimately, I see the Dow Jones dropping to at least 5000, but I can make a strong case for Dow 3000 before a real bottom is in place. And, if the global debt and currency crisis reaches the magnitude that I unfortunately see as quite probable, then we could even see the Dow quoted in triple digits.

When the debt and currency led implosion begins, and it appears that this may be the case even now with the sovereign debt crisis that is exploding throughout Europe, we might finally see the talking heads on CNBC wake-up to the reality of our rotten-to-the-core financial system – led by central banks around the world – truly a financial Frankenstein of unimagined creation. I see no true bottom in the global economy/stock markets taking place until 2013-2014, but it's likely going to be dramatically worse than any forecast you've been hearing in the main stream media. This is the reality that we should all prepare for, and this is also why it's no time to be a hero or to try and catch a falling knife (Wall Street lingo for buying investments on the way down). There will be a once in a lifetime opportunity to buy prime stocks and real estate at bargain prices in the not too distant future but for now, continue to make smart decisions for yourself, for your family, and for your business. Unfortunately, the worst is yet to come.

When I say *the worst*, I'm talking about more than just huge stock market drops. I also see social unrest in our future as the global economies continues to weaken substantially, unemployment hits depression-like record levels, and our bankrupt countries are forced to make very difficult decisions about their social and entitlement programs. In the US, when state, local and municipal governments (and schools) finally run out of "welfare state" money, a bear market in stocks will be just about the last thing people are worried about. If you want a preview of coming attractions in the United States all you have to do is take a look at what's been happening on the streets of Greece, Italy, France, Ireland and the U.K. It's impossible to predict exactly when the tipping point for social unrest will come, but for now make sure that your personal financial house is in order by keeping your debts low, controlling your spending, and making preparations for an economy that will take at least three years to recover.

Although the White House team of top economic experts continues to forecast a "jobless" recovery while they drug our comatose economy with printing-press dollars, others are finally starting to see the writing on the wall. In a spirited piece on *Minyanville.com*, Kevin Depew asks what might happen if Congress stopped all the bailouts. The likely result would be a huge drop in financial markets and a 30% stock plunge, followed by another huge wave of bankruptcies and layoffs. Times would be tough — *very* tough. On the other hand, he asks, what if Congress were to approve even *more* bailout money? Every penny of it would be quickly absorbed by a financial system already reeling from unprecedented debt. The likely result would be a huge drop in financial markets and a 30% stock plunge, followed by another huge wave of bankruptcies and layoffs. Times would be tough – *very* tough.

So, what's the difference? I'm glad you asked, because although the outcomes may appear identical at first, they're not. The difference is that *without* more bailouts, we'll return within about two to three years (give or take) to a healthier, stronger economy and companies that operate as if they're deeply responsible for their own business decisions. With continued bailouts we'll emerge from a lost decade with an economy and society crippled by the cost of bailing out businesses that operated with irresponsibility and a near total disregard for not just taxpayers but for their very own shareholders. This is it – the last chance to do the right thing.

But you and I already know how this story ends. The right thing will not be done. There will be more bailouts – and then more bailouts as we continue to write checks to failed companies. Meanwhile, once-healthy businesses face economic doom, cannibalized by zombie companies absorbing dollars that, had they been freely spent in a healthy system, would have been rightly theirs. We've become the bailout nation and look how it's been working out so far. Have you seen any new jobs yet?

Our system needs purging, and the balloon needs to be allowed to burst naturally. This will allow us to get this over with once and for all. Will it be painful? Yes, it absolutely will, at least for those that have made terrible decisions with their money for decades, if not an entire lifetime. This is how a free market system is supposed to work, and unless we allow the process to play itself out, we'll repeat the same mistakes that Japan has made for the last two decades while they attempted to prop up failed banks and a broken and corrupted corporate system. So, how has their economy and stock market done over this time frame? It's not pretty. Japan's stock market plummeted from a high of 38,000 to about 8000 before creeping back up to around 10,000 at the time of this writing. They've also experienced massive deflation, as evidenced by a real estate market that has dropped every single year for close to two decades.

Yet, for some reason we're determined to use the same playbook. As Albert Einstein said, *"Insanity is doing the same thing over and over again expecting a different result."* Massive government bailouts, printing our currency into oblivion and passing down $100 trillion in debt to our kids (and to their kids); now that's the definition of insanity. Do we really think that capitalism can be saved by socialism? One by one, US and global leaders are lining up to talk up their respective schemes to end this once in a lifetime economic collapse. Collectively they're putting on a unified road show to convince all of the "sheeple" that the trillions upon trillions being spent on massive, never-before-seen global bailouts are going to save us all from the oncoming freight train that is the Second Great Depression. Listen and please listen carefully; don't believe a single thing they are saying. If their lips are moving, they're lying.

Here's the truth of the matter. One by one, our largest and once most respected mega-companies are becoming insolvent, and there's absolutely nothing that can be done to stop the process.

The debt levels and derivatives held against this debt are just too overwhelming. We're now in a period of unmatched deleveraging, where bank financing is virtually impossible to obtain. From individuals to corporate America to the entire corporate world (outside of China), funding is simply unattainable. Remember when Circuit City had to liquidate because a buyer could not be found and additional financing was impossible? 30,000 employees lost their jobs practically overnight. Now, extend that same process to thousands of companies worldwide and you get an idea of how ugly things are about to become.

As I mentioned earlier, names that were once synonymous with corporate bedrock like AIG, Lehman, Countrywide, Merrill Lynch, Citi, Bank of America, and Bear Stearns (just to name a few) have either completely imploded or are in the final stages of the implosion process. Worldwide we're talking about $30 trillion in wealth that was destroyed in less than 12 months. It's nearly impossible to even fathom an outcome like this, isn't it? And next up are companies like GE and MGM. GE saw its market value drop from $500 billion to just $60 billion in a very short period of time and is literally days away from becoming a penny stock and one of our latest zombie mega-companies. MGM's share price dropped from over $100 to just $2 in a similarly short time span and will almost certainly face bankruptcy and liquidation in the coming crisis.

In the next year or two this sordid story will repeat itself over and over again. The money to fund our bankrupt system and "play now, pay later" lifestyle is gone and won't return for years.

"Later" is officially here. Our fearless (and powerless) leaders will continue to intervene and attempt to stop the bleeding with trillions of increasingly worthless paper dollars that our kids and grandkids will be on the hook to make good in the form of a crushing future tax burden. Just as we saw in the 1930s, these rescue efforts will not only fail, but will also indebt the next generations for decades to come. All the while the "sheeple" will listen to the rosy recovery forecasts and continue to fall in line and follow the spiral all the way down in lockstep. Make no mistake about it; this is the path we're on.

We've entered the worst economic crisis since the 1930s and unfortunately it will not end with a recession and a six month stock market shocker. Once the current wave of bear rallies end and reality begins to set back in, we'll find that the stock market has only begun to crack. In fact, many of us may not see new highs for the Dow Jones again in our lifetimes. Had we simply allowed scores of failed banks, a corrupt Wall Street, and a bloated, credit-driven corporate America the natural ability to sink or swim from the very beginning, this episode might have resolved itself naturally within two or three uncomfortable years.

Then (as if all this relatively "visible" intervention and manipulation weren't already bad enough) Bernie Madoff happened. When *that* story broke it was officially time to say goodbye to any possibility of an extended bear market rally. In case you've never seen the 1910 mug shot of Charles Ponzi (yes, he was a real guy), he looks a lot like a cross between movie actors Alfred Molina and Bobby Cannavale. Ponzi didn't really invent the financial trick that's named after him (Charles Dickens actually described one like it in the novel Little Dorrit decades before Ponzi was born) but in 1920 he was the first one to get caught doing it for really big money in the United States, so the name stuck. These schemes come in all varieties, but basically they're fraudulent investment operations where "investors" are paid returns not from any real profit earned, but out of their own money or from funds collected from newer victims – usually attracted by the promise of above-market returns.

In all cases, Ponzi schemes are doomed to collapse under their own weight because they demand an ever-increasing flow of new money to keep them going. In the extremely rare event that there are any earnings, they'll never begin to cover what's been paid in by the unsuspecting investors. Ponzi schemes ultimately fail in one of three ways. First, the perpetrator simply disappears with the accumulated cash before the fraud is discovered. Second, the scheme starts to collapse when the promoter has trouble paying out the promised returns and investor panic creates a "bank run" effect. Third, an unexpected market downturn (like the one that exposed Madoff) induces investors to start withdrawing funds, not because they've lost faith in the investment, but simply because of market fundamentals. At the risk of drifting off topic here, does any of this remind you of things you read about in the last two chapters?

Madoff's version of the Ponzi scheme stands as the largest financial investor fraud committed by a single person in history. Losses are estimated at roughly $30 billion, based on the money invested by his victims. Add in the promised returns and the losses skyrocket to nearly $65 billion. Bernard Madoff is living proof of a Ponzi scheme's ability to fool not just individual and institutional investors, but also securities authorities for a very long time. Madoff's claims that he started running the scheme singlehandedly in 1991, but prosecutors assert that it could go back more than 20 years involving numerous unnamed accomplices. What makes this case all the more alarming is that Madoff wasn't some shady fringe character with soft credentials. His firm had a track record dating back to the 1960s and he was a former NASDAQ chairman with high profile social, political and business connections.

I'm not trying to scare you. Well – yes I am, but not to death – just into action. The point I'm trying to make here is that if the system we trust with our money can allow someone like Bernie Madoff to prosper, even for a while, we need to be extremely selective about whom we trust, and we need to *educate* ourselves enough to know when something really is too good to be true! Just because a movie star you like smiles at you on TV in a $1,000 suit doesn't mean the company that hired him won't rob you blind if they get the chance. If you're counting on the SEC to protect you from these people, remember that they made more than one trip to Madoff's offices, qualified whistle blowers cried foul and he was *still* able to cover his tracks until the market dropped out from under him and brought the whole thing down by accident.

Besides the sheer size of it, here's why this particular incident is so relevant to our "Financial Frankenstein" overview.

Madoff's scheme had big money investors from all over the world aggressively clawing back funds from money managers and hedge funds and the result was massive new pressure on US and global stock markets. No one trusts anyone, and the financial world will never be the same again. Before this bear market is all over I predict that 70% of all hedge funds will be out of business and another $5 trillion will be pulled from equity investments along with them.

The really bad news here is that we're approaching index levels where bear markets begin rather than where bull markets get underway, so my forecasts going into the next decade are only going to get more pessimistic. Stock markets around the globe have been absolutely battered. This is once in a lifetime stuff and it's not nearly over yet. Here's the medium term problem – as defaults begin to pick up speed in the corporate debt and commercial properties markets, the banks will need more bailouts just to stay afloat. This is the big reason that they didn't lend out any of their newfound TARP money. They knew they were going to need this capital just to remain solvent.

Apart from all this, there are some other important reasons why the worst of the economy is still ahead of us, rather than behind us. The bad news from unemployment will continue to hit us for some time and I continue to believe it will "officially" reach 12-14% before it's all over. As I've told you before, the U-6 figure on unemployment is the only one that takes all the true data into account and it's already hovering around 17%. The next shoe beginning to drop is in commercial real estate and state and municipal debt, and we've already seen anchor tenants leaving malls and commercial properties in droves. This will continue on a scale we haven't seen in our lifetimes. Along with this, massive consumer debt will lead to a collapse of insolvent credit card companies, insurance providers and of course, collateralized auto loans. As with Ponzi schemes, these debt levels simply can't be sustained.

Now, as we established early in this book, everything really is connected. The economic engineering experiments we've talked about (and their unintended consequences) extend far beyond the immediate impacts we've described on Wall Street. We haven't even begun to cover the economic cancer called entitlements (Social Security, Medicare and Medicaid)! If you haven't seen the excellent movie *I.O.U.S.A.*, make sure you do. If you can't catch it at a local theater or documentary film festival, you can get it from rental services like Netflix. Here's the bottom line. Most people are blissfully unaware that most, if not all of the money that's supposed to be in the Social Security funds has already been borrowed to pay for other programs. The US has over 100 trillion in debt and just about 40 trillion in assets, which means that our government is officially bankrupt. In the future, our taxes will have to increase to 70-80% just to pay the interest on our massive debt and to pay for these bankrupt entitlement programs!

This is why I have a real issue with Warren Buffet's advice to buy stocks for the long term. Can you see stock prices going up in the future with taxes at 70%? I'm struggling with this one and with another Buffet issue as well. While the *New York Times* gladly ran his puff piece on the stock market, they conveniently left out the fact that he has over \$3 billion in stock market "derivatives losses" tied to S&P futures, and if the market continues to drop, his derivatives losses will only increase. Somehow, I think that people should have been informed of this. I've even read serious articles that push for an SEC investigation into Buffet over this. It's not likely to happen, but if it were you or me?

In an earlier chapter, I briefly touched on the work of Ludwig von Mises of the Austrian school of economics and the counterpoint he offered to a few of the more disastrous theories of John Maynard Keynes, known today as "Keynesian" economics. This would be a good point to explore some of the differences between these two schools of thought, because they're extremely relevant to our discussion of the misguided interventions our government and financial institutions continue to impose on the market. It turns out that a lot of the more destructive policies that are good for the corporatocracy but bad for the American people gain wide acceptance by exploiting fear. It's an old tactic of power addicts who are short on ethics.

Why does it work? There are four emotional stages that the majority of any population must endure when dealing with tough situations (and I would say that 17% real unemployment and the greatest level of poverty in close to two decades qualifies as pretty tough). Of course this is just in the United States. In Spain, the real unemployment rate is over 30% and in much of the rest of Europe (thanks to their own entitlement addictions) the real unemployment rate averages well over 20%. This same reality is setting in all over the world. A quiet discontent is creeping into the global mindset – a sense of anxiety that our kids may not have the same opportunities that we have enjoyed. The four stages are shock, denial, fear and acceptance.

In the spring of 2010, I predicted that we were close to coming out of denial and were about to enter the fear stage. In the fear stage, the reality of our dire situation will begin to sink in with more and more of the population. This is when stock markets retreat to new lows, homeowners realize that their property value will continue to decline for years to come, and economic desperation (for most) begins to set in. It turns out that we've remained in the denial stage longer than I thought we would and here's why. Those of us who have managed to hold onto our incomes are doing okay. For the fortunate ones among us, the economy seems to be holding on. Of course, tens of trillions in global government stimulus programs and loan guarantees (taxpayer funded bailouts) that mask economic realities can tend to have that effect.

This is Keynesian economics hard at work. Keynesian economics is the model recommended by economists like the very liberal Paul Krugman, whose Nobel economics prize is second only to Barack Obama's Nobel peace prize on the laugh-o-meter. Keynesian economics can best be described as the theory that *active government intervention in the marketplace is the best method of ensuring economic growth and stability.* Or as I like to say "I'm from the government and I'm here to help."

Here's the bottom line on economic theories. Liberals believe that the answer to a strong economy lies in the Keynesian approach, while conservatives believe in the Austrian school of economics, which teaches that the free market system (pure capitalism) is the only tried and true method of growing and sustaining a strong economy. Now, for the George W. Bush haters (and on many issues that includes me), who bought into the liberal message that Republican economic strategies are to blame for the mess we're in now, consider this. Under Bush we had the lowest unemployment rate in a generation. His mistakes with the housing market, defense spending, two wars and government bailouts for Wall Street and the banking industry were beyond atrocious, and without a doubt they helped to put us on the path to economic destruction.

But that doesn't mean that his belief in the Austrian school was a mistake. To the contrary, tax revenues were at a record high during his presidency. Bush succeeded in lowering the income tax rate for all Americans, yet somehow tax revenues to the government increased. This is the very definition of the Austrian school, yet for some reason almost no conservative can find their voice to make this point; *when income tax rates decline, corporate and personal profits increase – therefore the overall level of tax revenues must rise.* We saw precisely the same result under three presidents that lowered taxes; Republicans Ronald Reagan and Bush II and Democrat Bill Clinton. The problem of course was that they spent all of these record tax receipts incredibly poorly, with the help of a very complicit Democratic majority in Congress. The most critical point to grasp here is that *government spending* is the issue, not the Austrian school of economics.

Now let's return to the four emotional stages as they apply to the Keynesian vs. Austrian debate and the subject of denial.

Because the current administration is under the total control of Keynesian devotees (and yes, Bush's hands were just as dirty at the end of his presidency with the $890 billion TARP bailout), we are now witness to endless government bailouts and a level of economic intervention from Ben Bernanke's Federal Reserve that defies credibility. The same can be said for the behavior of all central banks globally.

When you flood tens of trillions in funny money into the economy, it has to go somewhere. In this case, it's going to the very same criminally operated banking cartels that caused this crisis in the first place. Sure, some of it is trickling down throughout the economy, but just barely enough to put off an official depression and keep the "sheeple" in denial — at least for a while longer. Intermittent reinforcement is one of the most powerful behavior modification tools ever invented — like a slot machine that pays out just enough to keep you playing.

You see, the haves are still making and spending money. Some of us still have our primary sources of income, and that allows us to support an economy that relies on 70% consumerism. But what happens when the funny money is gone and unemployment rises sharply for all, regardless of economic class? What happens when *everyone* realizes that their homes are continuing to drop in value with no end in sight, including the wealthy? What happens when the real economic crash takes place, like when the bond bubble pops and no one in the US or abroad is willing to buy debt from our bankrupt government anymore?

This new economic drama makes the FED even more desperate to re-inflate our bubble of an economy, and Bernanke is more determined than ever to print the world's reserve currency (the soon-to-be extinct US dollar) into oblivion. The currency war that is underway – this race to see who can devalue their currency faster than the other guy – is just getting started. After all, what better way to pay your debts than to simply print new dollars, and then use the fresh money to pay back creditors? Is this an approach you'd consider to be either legally or morally sound? I didn't think so. This is the financial engineering and manipulation I've been writing about for years, and because I believe in the economic laws of capitalism and free markets, I know the karma we have headed back our way is going to be overwhelmingly negative. In this case it will be hyperinflation, or maybe we should call it "karma-flation."

Anyone who can do basic math realizes that the same bleak economic reality facing the US lies directly ahead for Japan, Ireland, Spain, Portugal, Italy, Greece, every small European country, and ultimately for the UK. Can China, with its 60 million vacant homes, support the entire global economy? And, how will your country do, be it Canada, Australia, Germany, Sweden or Norway, when the rest of the world is competing for investors to buy their *own* government debt? Will you be able to bail the rest of civilization out? The remaining question for me is *when do we leave the denial stage and enter the fear stage?* And the best answer I can give you is that when it happens it will be too late to prepare.

I have warned about the coming reality as much as humanly possible over the last five years. This is why we own gold and silver. This is why we remain as intelligently debt free as possible. And this is why we reduce our exposure to the *old paradigm mindset*. Because once we reach the fear stage it will be too late. And then, once there's blood in the streets (another Wall Street adage), we'll be in a position to buy these very same assets at multi-generational lows. One of the best definitions of fear I've ever heard is "False Evidence Appearing Real." Prepare now and make this your definition as well. If this sounds really depressing, just remember that it doesn't have to be. The opportunities to prosper, even now, are as great, if not greater, than they've ever been (especially if you're an entrepreneur). This is why a recession serves such a major purpose. It gives us an opportunity to buy "real assets" at bargain basement prices so that when the economy begins to prosper once again, everything that we bought low, we can eventually sell high.

Here's the major problem facing us for the next 12 months plus. We live in a debt based society that uses borrowed money as its engine of growth. Without freshly issued debt, our economy MUST contract and it must do so until the excesses are purged from the system. This is why I continue to believe that this recession will be the worst of our lifetime. With regard to the stock market, the most important "take-away" here is this; the major driver of our economy is on life support and stocks by any long term valuation measures are still expensive.

As much as it hurts to write this (and I absolutely *hate* to write this) I believe the odds are 70/30 that we're headed into another Great Depression. There's not a whole lot that can be done about it. There's no official economic indicator or definition that proves we're headed into another depression, but it's obvious to anyone watching that things are about to get a whole lot worse. The stock market is a leading indicator, and this massive downward pressure we began to see in 2008 is telling us all that we need to know. As I've been saying, people are basically in denial because the economy has yet to really get hit.

For those that think my high gold and silver forecasts are outlandish, or that the FED, the US government and other governments and central banks around the world have a handle on things, please keep this one point in mind. The very same mad scientists that brought $700 trillion in weapons of mass financial destruction into existence in the form of completely unregulated derivatives; the very same people that pushed the world's entire financial system to the brink of systemic collapse one year ago; and the very same groups that first came up with the idea for a fiat currency system are the very same people that are in charge today. Whether it's this year or next, or possibly even three years from now, we *will* witness the next phase of the crash. And this time there won't be the money or the political will left to save us from ourselves.

CHAPTER SEVEN
MAGICAL MISDIRECTION –
WHERE ARE THE
PERP WALKS?

By now, after reading about all the financial engineering experiments gone wrong in our government and financial institutions, you might be asking yourself how all these things could be allowed to happen. How could all of the agencies, experts and elected officials entrusted with our protection miss all of these warning signs after the vivid and painful lessons we learned from the first Great Depression? As you'll see, I don't consider myself to be a conspiracy theorist, but I am convinced that criminal conflicts of interest have gone unpublicized and unpunished in our government and corporate systems for a very long time. In the next few pages, let's examine some of the clever corruption that has gradually disguised itself over the years as "business as usual."

You don't have to believe in large, complicated or ancient conspiracies to see that it's possible for a select few who have the means, motive and opportunity to "game the system" when the right loopholes present themselves. As you've already discovered in *CrashProof*, the way the Federal Reserve itself came into being from 1910 to 1913 (against major public and political opposition) proves it can be done. After years of painstakingly putting the right pieces of information and influence into place, it only took a handful of profit-minded powerbrokers and one or two self-interested friends on Capitol Hill to seize the moment and find a way around the will of the American people and their constitutionally elected representatives.

We might have been a lot easier to fool back in 1913, but how could anyone get something like that past us *today* under the public scrutiny of radio, television, the internet, a booming independent film community and the all-seeing eye of C-SPAN on cable? Actually, there are at least two ways to do it. The first way is to figure out how to control the media through interlocking board memberships and financial leverage. Did you know that the vast majority of news and information you and I consume is controlled by only six mega-corporations, and that media is just one several global cartels built to keep power in the hands of the elite? The second way is through a technique called *misdirection*. Psychologists and marketing experts know that human perception is highly selective. Without this important filtering ability we'd freeze up and daily information overload would make it impossible for us to think or act.

We voluntarily participate in misdirection all the time in pop culture. In fact, one Madison Avenue king is rumored to have said that "advertising is the art of arresting human intelligence long enough to get money from it." Entertainers like David Blaine, rock concert effects designers and famous filmmakers all know how to exploit our selective perception by drawing our attention to one place while the action they don't want us to notice is happening somewhere else. It was masterful use of misdirection that made the stunning plot twist (and six Oscar nominations) possible at the end of M. Night Shyamalan's film *The Sixth Sense*. Watch it a second time and you'll see a completely different movie. The clues were there in plain sight the whole time — we just didn't notice them because the director drew our eyes away from them with movement, lighting and camera techniques. Big money has been using exactly the same tricks since the Rothschild dynasty began in the 18th century, again, often with interlocking board memberships and borderless holding companies that make ownership and the true sources of influence virtually untraceable.

But who would do such a thing and how would they benefit from it? Thanks to filmmaker Oliver Stone's *JFK* and similar portrayals, Dwight D. Eisenhower will always be remembered as the grandfatherly presidential figure who warned us about the dangers of an expanding military-industrial complex and its potential to undermine our national sovereignty and individual liberties. It's rarely noted, however that Eisenhower was safely *out* of the Whitehouse and his beltway insider status before he blew the whistle on a system that he exploited and, in fact, helped to create during his administration. It's common knowledge and fully documented that many of his key advisors and appointees had overlapping personal and professional ties to the same multinational corporations with a financial stake in the outcome of world events today. Once again, you don't need to be a wild-eyed conspiracy theorist to at least give this idea some consideration – it's just one former fraternity brother helping another off the record when there's a large but ethically "questionable" profit to be gained.

Those who are familiar with John Perkins and his bestseller *Confessions of an Economic Hitman* know that corporate empire building in the name of US national interests is nothing new. Mr. Perkins is a frequent guest speaker at Wealth Masters events and is known for his balanced and scrupulously documented accounts of the international interventions he took part in along with technical "consulting" firms. In a nutshell, the "economic hitman" process he described involved cooking up official-looking economic, environmental and demographic studies (with grossly exaggerated upside forecasts) that encouraged leaders of third-world or developing nations to take on enormous "development" loans from the World Bank or the International Monetary Fund.

When these countries inevitably defaulted on these impossibly large debts, the economic hitmen would fly back in (this time as "rescuers") and offer to "renegotiate" the loans in return for the rights to the country's natural resources, blanket environmental waivers or any number of other "blank check" considerations that favored major US industries. Leaders who refused to play would mysteriously leave office for personal reasons or end up having unfortunate "accidents." When back page stories appeared about the US military showing up as "peacekeepers" or "advisors" in some backwater banana republic, that signaled an extremely rare failure on the part of the economic hitmen to close the deal. John's new book is called *Hoodwinked* and it contains a blow by blow account of the role multinational corporations (skating above or outside the bounds of governmental and legal constraints) played in the recent collapse of Iceland's economy. If any of these techniques sound oddly familiar to you, it's because they're in use today right here in our own backyard. What goes around comes around.

Here's why it's naïve and dangerous to underestimate the opportunistic agility of corporations that operate beyond the reach of sovereign governments. No one wants to dishonor the memories of the precious lives that were lost on September 11, 2001, but there were other losses that day that are eerily conspicuous by their absence in most main stream media accounts. Few people realize that included in the property that was destroyed forever when the World Trade Center towers fell, according to highly credible sources, was the largest single store of prosecution case files held by the US Securities and Exchange Commission.

To put the implications of this into chilling perspective, consider for a moment that these documents not only included crucial (and irreplaceable!) evidence in major financial corruption cases like Enron and WorldCom, but also government-sealed inquiries into dealings of government and corporate fraud at the highest levels – some dating back as far as the 1920s. Building 7, where many of these sensitive records were kept, was situated on the city block just north of the World Trade Center complex and became only the third steel building in history (before or since 9/11) to collapse from fire damage. You probably already know that the other two were the north and south towers of the World Trade Center. And for those that have either forgotten or may have never known in the first place, Building 7 – forty seven stories tall – fell to the ground later that day in just over six seconds. And no, Building 7 was not hit by a plane.

Strangely enough, numerous independent sources report that any building in the immediate area that was not owned by Silverstein Properties (who allegedly cleared $500 million profit on the WTC 7 insurance claim) remained standing. FEMA, NIST and other investigating agencies confirm that no firefighters or emergency personnel had occupied the building for hours before the collapse. No conspiracy theory is required to seek answers to any number of questions about the many strange coincidences of that fateful day. Questions like; why were no military fighter jets scrambled in time to intercept any of the four hijacked aircraft? How did hijackers with suspiciously little aviation training manage to fly such highly detailed and complex flight patterns? And exactly how did office fires (which physically cannot melt steel) bring down two 100-story-plus buildings and a forty seven-story building, all at free fall speed and directly into their own footprints?

Without knowing exactly who could have done something this unimaginable and horrendous, my years of financial training have taught me that *following the money* will at least steer you in the right direction. And while *CrashProof* is certainly not an investigative look into 9/11, one of my goals in writing this book is to encourage people to begin *asking the tough questions*. Remember, there are no stupid questions, only stupid answers, and if asking tough questions makes you a conspiracy theorist, then I am proud to be just that. Or as I like to say, I'm proud to be an equal opportunity offender and look forward to adding you to this contrarian-thinking mastermind group. Unfortunately, we live in an age of megalomaniacs, and without sounding paranoid, it pays to understand that groups or individuals with the right motivation and enough money and influence, can and do try to exercise massive amounts of control.

In fact, "false flag" operations have been common practice in international conflicts since the days of Sun Tzu. Authenticated memoranda pre-dating the Cuban Missile Crisis document false flag scenarios planned and funded by covert elements of the military and intelligence communities that were strangely similar in concept and execution to the 9/11 disaster. You don't have to be a fringe "inside job" theorist to see how even loosely organized resources and "happy accidents" could be exploited for their collateral benefits to industrial and banking giants arming and funding both sides of any given world conflict – corporations who also happen to have large investments and property holdings to protect in those war-torn areas. Even so, consider carefully that many unanswered questions still linger today about events like the Reichstag Fire, Pearl Harbor, the Gulf of Tonkin Incident, and the shooting of JFK. The truth is out there and it's more than okay to ask the tough questions. The rock group *The Clash* may have summed it up best with their now famous line "there ain't no Russians and there ain't no Yanks, just corporate criminals playing with tanks."

Back to a different kind of corruption. Insider trading happens every single day – only the unlucky few get caught. Does it really take such a leap of faith or reason to suppose that elite captains of the industrial and financial worlds with access to highly privileged information could manipulate these kinds of events to their advantage (even if they didn't have to instigate them) from behind an international veil of untraceable assets and partnerships? And as they use misdirection to enslave vast segments of the world population under massive and irreconcilable debt, we're all complacently looking the other way at CNN, *Dancing with the Stars, Jersey Shore* and a dozen channels of ESPN.

When you put all these puzzle pieces together, a very disturbing pattern starts to emerge. This is why the criminal convictions I've written about so many times will probably never happen – at least not under the paradigm we've accepted so blindly in the past. Oh, sure, a token handful of expendable top-echelon folks like Ken Lay or Bernie Madoff fall in show trials that play to the public's short-lived sense of moral outrage ("Thank heaven that Martha Stewart is finally behind bars where she belongs – hey, is *American Idol* on tonight?"). But the vast majority of mission-critical players needed to keep the multinational corporations running as they have for decades (if not centuries) will continue to operate anonymously in the shadows — out of the public eye and beyond the reach of any court of law.

Again, this is not in any way a new development, but business as usual. It should not surprise you to learn that a number of the prosecuting authorities who made key decisions during the Nuremburg trials were among the documented legal, political and corporate players who not only helped plan and fund the industrial interests behind the Nazi war effort in WWII, but in many cases also assisted in the transfer of Nazi assets, technology and personnel away from public scrutiny after the war. Many decision makers in key government positions on both sides of the war shared connections (and profit motives) through major law firms, banks and even foreign subsidiaries of German industrial giants like I.G. Farben, Thyssen and Siemens. We can see that things haven't changed all that much in the halls of power in the last 100 years.

So, with all this background in mind, let's return to our original question about the current economic crisis; *how could this happen?* It's not a failure of capitalism or the free market system. It's because of the way we've gradually allowed the system to become corrupted by criminal conflicts of interest, one compromise at a time. Now let's take a more specific look at a few of these corrupt activities and see how the consequences have begun to snowball over time. We're going to be jumping around a bit from one subtopic to another, so bear with me.

For many years, Wall Street was placing enormous bets on risky debt obligations called derivatives. I've been writing about derivatives for years, and these weapons of mass financial destruction finally succeeded in popping the bubble that was the US economy. The con was so massive that it took the rest of the world down with it. Think about this for a moment. Goldman Sachs (home of former Treasury Secretary Henry Paulson) and JP Morgan, along with several of Wall Street's most prestigious firms engineered the very derivative instruments that got us into this mess in the first place. Then, they pocketed hundreds of billions in profits along the way.

As I mentioned in the last chapter, the top executives from these failed companies (Bear Stearns, AIG, Lehman, and others) had *no* skin in the game. Collectively they owned less than 1% of the outstanding shares in their firms, so they had absolutely nothing to lose. All they had to do was get legislation passed that would allow the investment and banking industries to use leverage of 40 to 1 – up from the already insanely large norm of 10 to 1 that came to be accepted under the FED's hare-brained "fractional reserve" scheme. Along with the creation of financial derivatives that had little to no backing, they engineered record profits out of thin air, which in turn allowed them to be compensated with billions upon billions in obscene bonuses.

So, the real question is; how is it that none of these con artists ended up in court along with the likes of Bernie Madoff? So far the government has thrown away approximately $10 trillion of taxpayer money to bail out these crooks and we've yet to see a single perp walk. Now, trillions in losses are hitting Main Street right between the eyes and it's clear that we're facing the most devastating financial crisis in more than 80 years. Criminal exploitation of derivatives were a huge contributing factor, combined with the fact that colossal stimulus spending, zero interest rates, over two trillion in toxic debt/government debt purchased by the FED, and the loosest monetary policy in history have done absolutely nothing to revitalize the economy. It's no surprise to Austrian school economists that these Keynesian policies have been an unqualified failure.

Here's why derivatives were so devastating. It's common knowledge that the US no longer makes anything – not really anyway. Most of that "stuff" is imported now. Soon, we'll have the Big Two instead of the Big Three, and you can pretty much write off close to half of all US industries that are manufacturing related. So, what's been driving our economy for the last ten years? Approximately 38% of our GDP now comes from the financial industry, and it's safe to say that this represents at least 50% of all corporate profits in the US. Think about this for a moment – more than half of all corporate profits come from an industry that now caters almost exclusively to the "elites." We've come a long way from the "Greatest Generation" that won WWI and WWII, and then went on to build the most dominant industrial era in the planets history.

In today's "plastic generation" Wall Street, banks, hedge funds, insurance and credit card companies have become the life-blood of our economy. For at least a decade the use of derivatives, which are nothing more than financial engineering gone haywire, allowed an already out of control industry to become up to fifty times more leveraged than ever before – because that's where the short term profits and mega bonuses were made possible. Derivatives, such as hedges on crops for farmers, or oil and natural gas hedges used in the energy industry make perfect sense. They actually serve a needed purpose. However, allowing the AIG's of the world to create financial derivatives using extreme leverage in order to boost the bottom line, earn obscene bonuses and move the CEO to employee income ratio to a never before seen 400 to 1, could only make sense in the glory days of Rome – just before the fall.

Because derivatives actually turned out to be the "weapons of mass financial destruction" Warren Buffet predicted they'd be in 2004, we've now lost our primary engine of growth. In less than nine months Lehman, Merrill, AIG, Bear, Fannie, Freddie, Countrywide, WAMU, and 90% of all mortgage companies were wiped out. It's still hard to believe this actually happened. In fact, as we established in the last chapter, it's clear that most people are still in denial about what this is going to mean to us in the long term. Rest assured, much like the Roman Empire, where making money on money became the industry of choice, the $700 trillion market in unregulated derivatives will have devastating ramifications.

We've only begun to scratch the surface of the web of interlocking conflicts of interest that plague the globes financial systems. The *American News Project* published a report on the economic crisis and the subprime lending schemes. The report mentioned that many foreclosures were being pursued by Litton Loan Servicing, a company owned by Goldman Sachs. That's right – former Treasury Secretary Henry Paulson's Goldman Sachs. Litton was a leader in the field known as subprime servicing, which specialized in the handling of subprime mortgages where the homeowner had fallen behind in payments and was at risk of foreclosure. In other words, they were a type of collection agency focusing on people that were about to be kicked out of their homes. Litton has frequently been accused of engaging in abusive practices, including more than 100 lawsuits in federal court since the beginning of 2004.

In December of 2007 Goldman Sachs bought the company for $428 million, plus repayment of $916 million of outstanding Litton debt. Goldman, which probably didn't want the world to know of its buyout, never issued so much as a basic press release about the transaction. Was Hank Paulson's delay in offering meaningful help to struggling homeowners an effort to help Goldman's Litton operation? The bigger question is; why weren't we told about this relationship and why wasn't there any investigation into the issue, along with Goldman's role in the very derivatives that spawned this crisis in the first place? In case you didn't know, Hank Paulson made all of his hundreds of millions while running Goldman Sachs. That was his job before being anointed as Treasury Secretary (the next Goldman genius that would save us all).

What everyone should know is that Goldman was a major player in the creation of most of the derivatives that led to our debt implosion and severe recession, namely credit default swaps or CDS. CDS act as insurance, and allow you to bet against the future of a company – or of a country – and were widely used to push companies into insolvency beginning in early 2008 with the Bear Stearns blow-up. Speculators shorted Bear Stearns stock while buying CDS on Bear Stearns at the same time. It's been widely reported that Goldman Sachs made huge profits on Bear Stearns rapid implosion, as did JP Morgan, which then wound up buying Bear Stearns at fire-sale prices.

That same CDS playbook was then used time and again to bring down one company after another in the fourth quarter of 2008, and just as CDS were being used to punish the share prices of Goldman and JP Morgan to the point of no return, good old Hank Paulson came to the rescue of Goldman – his former company – with the $850 billion bailout called TARP. Paulson has admitted that he got down on his knees and begged Congressional leaders for the bailout, claiming that the financial system as we know it would be lost without it. What he really meant was that his old employer would be lost, along with the all-powerful JP Morgan, and that just could not be allowed to happen. And with that, TARP had done its job. It came just a bit too late to help the likes of Bear and Lehman, and just in time to save companies like Goldman, JPM and AIG – the White Shoe Boys – as Gerald Celente would call them.

Multiple times in VRA updates I wrote that until we had a "perp walk" with these criminals in handcuffs, there was little chance of public confidence being restored. When it became public knowledge that Warren Buffet lost $9 billion in one quarter due to his own bad derivatives bets on the stock market there was a glimmer of hope that he would lead the charge for some kind of criminal investigation. But of course, Buffet knew the risks, and instead took action to profit from the ensuing financial collapse – which is why you don't hear Buffet calling derivatives Weapons of Mass Financial Destruction these days. At one point he suffered losses of up to 45% in his portfolio, however his insider connections and back room deals are helping to turn all that around. Invest like Buffet? Sure, but only if you're worth a cool billion or more. In other words, forget about it!

And the rigged game continues, and not just in New York. Quietly (and it's pretty amazing that this happened quietly) our current administration in Washington hijacked the rule of law. If you think I'm exaggerating, ask any qualified attorney who understands bankruptcy litigation. Chrysler's bondholders (the same investors that risked approximately $20 billion on the survival of the company) were told that they could take their legal claims to company assets and shove them where "the sun don't shine." Believe it or not, the United Auto Workers Union, (UAW) whose actions over the years contributed heavily to the company's collapse, was actually given senior status over the bondholders in bankruptcy court.

In case you're wondering; no, this has never happened before, and here's why this is such a big deal. The US has always presented itself as a country that honors the rule of law – a country that honors contracts – a country that prides itself on being the standard bearer for the world when it comes to respect for the legal system. Think about it this way; when the AIG bonus issue arose, President Obama said, *"we are a country that abides by the rule of law and a contract is a contract. Therefore we cannot interfere with the previously agreed to bonuses at AIG."*

So, it would appear that by Obama's logic, it's okay to abandon the rule of law when it comes to investors (in this case the Chrysler bondholders that had a fiduciary responsibility to the pensions, 401k and mutual funds they manage) but *not* for those who received billions in ill-gotten gains at AIG. I guess we now have to add double standards and situational ethics to the list of reasons why our economic system is headed for total collapse. Serious people are talking about this as possibly the most important challenge to our legal system in decades. Next up? If Obama isn't careful, and I mean very careful, he'll turn the US into a banana republic – a country that changes the law whenever it suits their purposes. I'm afraid that we've already crossed that line.

But legal threats aren't the only assault on public trust. Cooking the books is another time-honored tradition, not just on Wall Street, but in Washington D.C. as well. There's a big difference between what government statistics report and what's going on in the real world. Several readers commented on an update I wrote about GD2 (or the coming repeat of the great depression), saying that it was "too depressing." They asked if things could really get that bad again. Well, for one thing, you've got to remember that the numbers we're getting from the government now cannot be trusted. Figures may not lie, but liars can certainly figure.

One major case in point is the "official" reporting of unemployment figures. For many years I've quoted John Williams of *shadowstats.com*. Casey Research is another good data source. These people are among the few who make an effort to inject some reality and integrity into the murky (and easily manipulated) world of statistics. According to U-3 figures from the US Bureau of Labor Statistics, the unemployment rate is currently 9.8%. However, the real number, the U-6 figure, which includes those that have been out of work for more than a year, along with those working part time because they can't find a full time job, is now over 17%. That's right — if you're still discouraged and jobless after 1 year, the government conveniently ignores you in its calculations — how heartwarming. When a government official assures you our situation isn't close to the 20% unemployment we suffered in the Great Depression, keep the true U6 figures in mind. Numbers like these are leading to civil unrest, something that I predict will only increase as social services and food banks continue to be pushed to the breaking point.

Here's another reason why few trust the powers that be. According to the government, annual inflation is running at just 3%. This, of course, is a completely bogus number because food and energy were both removed from official inflation statistics a few years ago. Honestly, do you know *anyone* who doesn't include food or energy in their household budget? Adding these two "must haves" back into the formula where they belong gives us an annual inflation rate greater than 10%. This is what a greatly devalued dollar does to your purchasing power. The currency inflation we are beginning to experience today is an early warning sign that everyone should pay very close attention to. Trusting the government for accurate accounting on *anything* is becoming increasingly difficult, and this is why knowledge of history is so vitally important. Runaway hyperinflation — due to a collapsing currency — brought down Germany, Argentina, Russia and Zimbabwe. Those that believe it cannot happen to them typically share the same fate — and almost always sooner than later.

From the inception of the VRA eight years ago, I've warned about the dangers of the global fiat currency system (paper currencies backed by nothing of real value) along with the never ending issuance of debt at all levels (federal, state, municipal, corporate and consumer) which when combined have bankrupted what was once the most financially powerful country on the planet. I've shared my predictions onstage at venues around the world, and wherever WMI has traveled. In our m¹ Masters Program back in 2005 we predicted essentially every event that has taken place over the last five years, and especially since the bear market and recession began in earnest in September of 2008. I've been consistent in this message and I've been accurate — painfully so — because 90% of the events I've warned specifically about have taken place.

But I've missed things as well, and here is one that I missed, and missed big time. I seriously underestimated the devastation that US and global governments were willing to bring our way as the result of throwing trillions of freshly printed currency into their economies. Their view? It was necessary in order to keep our bubble of an economy inflated. Even though I knew that FED Chairman Bernanke was a self proclaimed "master student" of the Great Depression, the idea that our government would embark on the kind of reckless monetary policies that we're witnessing today simply never entered my mind. Sure, I heard Helicopter Ben tell us that he would drop dollars from the sky in order to prevent deflation, but like most, I thought this was idle chatter – wrong! Folks, we're talking about trillions in wild, amazingly ill-conceived taxpayer funded stimulus programs and government/ FED backed loans, and many trillions more bailing out the very same companies that created and infected the global economy with $700 trillion in planet killing derivatives. Mark my words; years from now our kids (and their kids) will curse Bernanke and Greenspan's very existence. I'm never 100% sure of anything, but this prediction is about as certain as any I've ever made.

With the government's tacit permission (not to mention our own silence and complacency) we've sat back and allowed the FED, along with central banks globally, to bankrupt our future. Coming in the near future (which could be anywhere from three months to three years) we'll learn that all of this government intervention was for naught, and that it actually made the situation many times worse than it otherwise would have been. Incredibly, a whopping 40% of our economy now comes from taxpayer funded stimulus programs, and once this money is blown, a very harsh reality is waiting for the unprepared, which now includes $100 trillion in unmanageable debt, hyperinflation and skyrocketing interest rates.

Truly, our children and their children will rightfully ask what the hell we were thinking. Why didn't we simply allow bankrupt companies to go bankrupt? Why didn't we allow the natural deleveraging process to take place? Why didn't we maintain a sound monetary system, backed by gold, which would have prevented all of this misery from happening in the first place? We raise our kids to make good decisions – to think things through clearly and only then to take informed action. Instead, history will prove us to have been the ultimate hypocrites for our own economic choices. Making matters worse, the absence of *honest* government supervision or regulation has increased the fear, mistrust and confusion that plague our financial markets – and our society – today.

You'll recall that earlier in this chapter I mentioned that most of the main stream media is controlled by only six mega-corporations. To be completely fair, because of the "sheeple" they've become, it's hard to hold the public's feet to the fire for either making or supporting bad decisions if they're not being given honest information. Why do so many important stories seem to just disappear? When the news finally did break (because it was too big to suppress anymore) about the multi-billion dollar Ponzi Scheme Bernie Madoff engineered over a 20 to 30 year period, I knew the story rang a bell. I went back through my files and found the original 2001 *Barron's* article by Erin Arvedlund. Her excellent research included quotes from several well known Wall Street veterans who openly questioned Madoff's ability to consistently generate 15% plus returns, year after year, in good markets or bad. Nobody was doing that well in options, trading the way Madoff traded.

All of the warning signs were there, and lots of bright people believed that this guy was running a huge scam. They were right, but no one seemed to care. After I looked up the original story I contacted Erin about the article and found her comments to me most interesting. *"After I wrote the article, nothing happened,"* she said. *"No one contacted me from the SEC or anything. I found that pretty strange – the story just died."* How many more Madoffs are out there? I've been writing about the vast conflicts of interest on Wall Street for years. Having spent 15 years in that industry I witnessed similar things on a regular basis, yet it's rare to see anyone held accountable or witness any real changes taking place in the investment business. And we wonder why investors are pulling their money out of the stock market (30 consecutive weeks as I write this). Just as we wonder why we have lost a generation of potential investors into the markets. Can we blame them?

While we're on the subject of investor confidence, please understand that Madoff's claim that he ran this gigantic fraud by himself is 100% unbelievable. There's simply no way that one man could have cranked out thousands of statements every month, not to mention keeping track of the comings and goings of billions of dollars without help – and lots of it. Madoff clearly had partners in crime, but as of this writing he went off to federal prison without naming any of them. So, the *Wall Street Journal* asks its readers, *"Could your investment manager be another Bernard Madoff?"* If someone like Mr. Madoff can do what he did right under the noses of the investment community, the media and the SEC and manage to get away with it for several decades, can investors anywhere sleep easy?

Ordinarily, when you pick an investment manager or financial planner, you're given some common-sense advice. Avoid managers who are unknown, unregulated, haven't been in the industry long or come without good referrals. But none of these selection criteria would have saved you from Mr. Madoff. As I mentioned earlier, he had tons of high level referrals, was respected on the Street as a former NASDAQ chairman and had been in business since 1960. Now that the cat is out of the bag, the SEC has no choice but to admit that "it did not do its job." Really? Tell us something we don't already know! When corruption at this level goes undetected and unpunished for such an inexcusably long time, there's no way that the average person has any hope of telling the good guys from the bad guys.

Speaking of accountability, numerous inquiries have been addressed to the FED to find out where all of the bailout money has gone. US Treasury and FED officials have repeatedly refused to disclose any information to the taxpayers who funded the bailouts. In a statement to the House Financial Services Committee, FED chairman Ben Bernanke said, *"Some have asked us to reveal the names of the banks that are borrowing, how much they are borrowing, what collateral they are posting. We think that's counterproductive."* Amazing, isn't it? Our money is being thrown away and we aren't even allowed to see who's getting it. Finally, adding insult to injury, CitiGroup, having been bailed out with your tax dollars, still spent over $400 million on naming rights for a sports stadium. You seriously could not make a story like this up.

Of course, they believe there's a good reason for all this secrecy. The powers that be desperately require the Federal Reserve to keep interest rates at artificially low levels, and to keep the economic house of cards from falling down, they must do so indefinitely. However, it will be impossible for them sustain this variation of the Ponzi scheme without creating a huge outbreak of inflation in the prices of food, energy, clothing, and just about everything else that people need to live and survive. Simply put, in order to prevent hyperinflation, we need interest rates to be higher than the rate of inflation. This, along with the demands of the creditors holding US debt is why rates have nowhere to go but up.

Recently, those that believe in Keynesian economics have been bragging about the possibility that Congress will run a deficit of "only" $1.5 trillion this year. They've issued dire proclamations about a replay of the 1937-1938 Depression within the Great Depression. White House favorite and number one Keynesian on the planet, Paul Krugman (unbelievably a Nobel Economics Prize winner) declared that *not* borrowing an additional $100 billion to hand out to the unemployed for another 99 weeks would surely plunge the country into recession again.

In support of his argument, here's the case he made (with a straight face) to a major metropolitan newspaper: *"Suddenly, creating jobs is out, inflicting pain is in. Condemning deficits and refusing to help a still-struggling economy has become the new fashion everywhere, including the United States, where 52 senators voted against extending aid to the unemployed despite the highest rate of long-term joblessness since the 1930s. Many economists, myself included, regard this turn to austerity as a huge mistake. It raises memories of 1937, when F.D.R.'s premature attempt to balance the budget helped plunge a recovering economy back into severe recession."*

So did Roosevelt's attempt to balance the budget in 1937 really cause the second major downturn in 1938? I prefer to verify what's being peddled to me by any economist, but especially when it's coming from Paul Krugman. Keynesian policies failed during the Great Depression, and they're failing today. An economic catastrophe caused by loose monetary policies, crushing levels of debt, and appalling lending practices cannot be solved by looser monetary policies, obscene debt obligations, or scenarios where the government commands banks (or "commandeers" as in the case of Fannie and Freddie) to make more bad loans.

I never imagined I'd live to see the Federal Reserve buy over $2 trillion of our own debt, but that's exactly what has happened. So far, the FED has purchased over $1 trillion in toxic mortgage-backed securities and over a trillion in US government debt, making the FED the largest holder of US debt, having just surpassed China. I think I need to say it once more so that the idea really sinks in (as much for me as for you); the Federal Reserve, a US-based cabal of international bankers, has become the lender of last resort to our own country. Seriously, can anyone reading this tell me that this Matrix-like economic science fiction makes any kind of sense whatsoever?

What makes this situation even more disturbing is that almost no one in the main stream media is making a big deal of this unprecedented level of criminality. There are still a few voices of reason out there making a laudable effort to put some realistic counterpoint on the airwaves. Among them are Glenn Beck, Dylan Radigan and our very own Wayne Allyn Root, one of America's most successful and ethical media personalities and entrepreneurs. In addition, Wayne is also a strong fiscal conservative, a leading figure in the national Libertarian party and serves as Senior Economic Advisor to Wealth Masters International. Wayne's best seller *The Conscience of a Libertarian* is now out in paperback and I highly recommend that you buy several copies, for yourself, your friends and your family.

Why isn't there more resistance to all this corruption? As this outrageous national scandal worsens, our Founding Fathers must be beyond rolling over in their graves — they're probably ready to rise up out of them with weapons in hand. Imagine a scene from *Paranormal Activity II*, but with Thomas Jefferson as the protagonist ghost leading the charge against Ben Bernanke and his global banking cronies. Now *that's* a movie I'd pay to see! I first read the following quote from Jefferson in 1999, about the same time that I met G. Edward Griffin and read his instant classic on money creation and the evils of the FED, *The Creature from Jekyll Island*. In an 1816 letter to John Taylor (senator and original Libertarian and states' rights supporter), Jefferson said *"I sincerely believe that banking establishments are more dangerous than standing armies."*

It was this quote that pretty much sealed the deal for me. I'd always felt that the FED and the US banking system would eventually bring this great country down, and Jefferson's wisdom from centuries ago convinced me of this. Like the predictions of pre-crime in the Tom Cruise futuristic thriller *Minority Report*, Jefferson was blessed with the ability to predict – and to warn about the future. Fast forward to 2011, and in my estimation, we're less than three years away from this bleak eventuality. You see, the Founders understood the importance of honest money and tried to protect our money from the bankers. A review of our nation's economic history reveals that bankers, in concert with a handful of traitors in Congress who were susceptible to graft, gained control of the monetary system, set up private "national" banks, began implementing mechanisms of usury and were then taken down, not once but twice.

President Andrew Jackson brought the nation to within about $32,000 of solvency after decommissioning "The Second Bank of the United States" (1818-1836) and restoring Congressional control of our money. It took the bankers another 70 years to buy their way back into Congress to control the creation and issuance of America's money. Then as I described in chapter four, the Federal Reserve was commissioned in 1913 through a series of corrupt manipulations by key members of Congress in cahoots with the Robber Barons. Again, read Mr. Griffin's most excellent book for complete details on this sad chapter in American history.

Since that time, the purchasing power of the dollar has been in steady decline (at least 95%), the hard assets of the nation have been in transition to the international bankers and governments are increasingly indebted to an unelected, international banking cabal that our own Congress commissioned to manage the US monetary system. We're staring over the edge of the financial abyss, and if our elected officials don't know that protecting America's money from these international bankers is part of the sacred trust we've given them, they're not worthy to represent our interests in government. By extension, that means that almost every sitting member of Congress is either a traitor or an ignoramus – and I choose both. If we have any chance of saving the US (not to mention the global financial system and our way of life) it's going to require a massive uprising from us – *We The People.*

And because Jefferson was right – because the international bankers *have* garnered more power than standing armies – the odds are slim to none that this implosion can be avoided. It's simply gone too far. This is why I have owned gold and silver, and recommended the purchase of same, since 2002. This is why I am short the stock market. This is why I am short government bonds. And this is another big reason why Karl Bessey and I founded Wealth Masters International. Of course, with this government and this FED, it has become increasingly difficult to make the timely and reliable predictions that are possible in a normal, free market economy. What we have now is not just socialism; it's actually state capitalism, which is exactly what China practices. Anyone who doesn't find this alarming is most likely a poorly informed socialist – at best.

So, let's try to pull all these interconnected threads together and draw some conclusions from them. If this overview of corruption in our financial systems has seemed a little rambling, it's because the extent and complexity of these criminal activities has reached a level never before seen in history. I can't tell you of a single investment or political expert I trust that feels the rule of law actually prevails in the United States any longer. When you have the depth of blatant financial criminality we've experienced over the last five years, with none of its major players in prison, much less even charged or indicted (and no, Madoff doesn't count), then I can tell you with a great deal of confidence that we're lost. Our Founding Fathers would not recognize the country they risked their very lives to create.

Is this reversible? Can we do something to right the ship? I imagine that sufficient numbers of new faces in Washington, with their hearts and minds in the right place, could possibly make this happen. But the wounds are much deeper than just simple financial crimes. What's the real issue? We've lost our moral high ground, which was the real reason that the United States was able to experience the most impressive growth and global power since the rise of the Roman Empire. How did we lose it? You won't hear the facts in the main stream media.

Consider this; the *wikileaks.org* document dump of real statistics on the war in Iraq exposed credible estimates that two out of three people killed (murdered) in Iraq have been innocent citizens. That means that anywhere from 100,000 to as many as 1 million innocent men, women and children have been needlessly killed by America's military machine. And we wonder why they hate us? Is it truly because our way of life and commitment to freedom is so abhorrent to them (as the military-industrial rationalization goes), or could it be that in our "righteous war on terror" we've also slaughtered innocent people simply because they happen to have been born in the wrong country and found themselves in the path of a greed-driven tornado?

Here's the way I've explained the consequences of this to both of our sons; "years from now, you'll almost certainly have enemies your age from the Middle East (and elsewhere likely) who hate, despise and want to kill you, simply because you're a child of my generation – the one that cost them the lives of people they deeply loved." As difficult as it might be to confront this hard truth, these are the roots of the terrorist threats we're likely to face for the rest of our lives and the rest of our children's lives. What I find deeply discouraging about this reality is that I know of no way to cure this kind of generational hatred.

For those who may think this perspective is anti-American or poorly reasoned, reverse the roles for a moment and imagine how your orphaned children might feel toward invaders of your home country in this exact scenario. As a result of all these double standards, the world will ultimately decide that the US dollar can no longer stand as the world's reserve currency. When that happens – and it won't be long from now – the end game will be clear to all. We've lost the privileges and benefits that come from earning the moral authority to lead, and this loss will result in a fall very similar to that of the Roman Empire.

CHAPTER EIGHT
REAL ESTATE AND THE ECONOMY – MORE DELEVERAGING

Mark Twain and Will Rogers are both remembered for giving similar words of advice. *"Buy land. They aren't making it anymore."* I wonder what their common sense recommendation would be today on all the taxpayer money going into the purchase of toxic assets left over from the subprime lending wreckage in the real estate market. I began publishing warnings about the great housing and real estate bubble in 2005, about one year before prices began to plummet, first on the coasts and then around the rest of the country. In spite of all the happy talk we kept hearing from real estate flippers and the FED, I stuck to my contrarian view that the artificial highs simply could not last against the coming debt implosion and onset of the deleveraging process. Odds (not to mention plain old common sense) were favoring a devastating decline. With the risk of a 50% price drop, I cautioned everyone about the dangers of being highly leveraged in real estate and encouraged folks to rethink their portfolios. When I see all the pain in the market today, I wish I'd been wrong – and today I wish I could say that the worst is over – but unfortunately that's not the case.

Currently we're seeing a temporary lull in mortgage defaults, but this is about to begin changing rapidly. All the signs are there and all the conditions are in place for the next shoe to drop, both in residential as well as commercial real estate. Each major class of mortgages from subprime to Option ARM to Alt-A will soon begin resetting in record numbers. The resets won't peak until late 2011, putting massive pressure on an already comatose housing market. What makes this especially troubling is the continued hemorrhaging that's taking place in the job market. Unemployment figures for the US are approaching levels we haven't seen since the Great Depression and we're seeing the same scenario play out globally.

These lost jobs are having the same "multiplier effect" that turned a temporary stock market bust into a decade-long downturn in the 1930s. It might interest you to know that the same thing happened in Japan during their "lost decade" (now turning into *two* lost decades) that saw their stock market drop by 80% Today's record-setting job losses are having the same effect here, which is why the administration is so desperate to jump-start the economy. What they don't understand is that the cure they're experimenting with (record levels of debt) is even worse than the disease. By the time they figure this out it will be too late. Huge debt levels + massive amounts of additional debt = insolvency and bankruptcy.

The worst is far from over, so to get clear on where we're going, it's important to take a look back at where we've been and how we got where we are today. These are some of the original concerns I raised with our Wealth Masters members and in my early VRA updates. As prices continued to rise, everyone believed that real estate was the one place to have your money. Almost every self-proclaimed guru out there had some type of real estate program they were marketing that was sure to make you a millionaire. If history has taught us anything, it's that when the majority believes prices must continue to go up, that's when it's time to sell.

There were several factors that were causing me to question the "conventional wisdom" at the time. The first thing that concerned me was just the basic economics of the situation. The market reached a point where fewer and fewer people could afford to buy a median priced home. This was the first sign of the bubble. The second thing that concerned me was that most of the ones who *were* still buying went in with next to nothing down, regardless of their credit score or debt-to-income ratios. They were using leverage like never before to play the rental property or "fix it and flip it" game. The third and most important thing that concerned me was the popular belief that real estate prices simply could not fall.

Japanese buyers thought exactly the same thing in the late 1980s and they're still suffering terribly as a result. Back in 2004, the *Financial Times* reported that residential real estate prices in central Tokyo rose by nine tenths of 1%. The reason such a ridiculously small increase made the headlines is because it was first time in 17 years that Tokyo property values went up at all. Back in the late 1980s Japanese speculators were just as delusional about ever increasing prices as Americans were at the height of the bubble in places like Arizona, California, Nevada and the Florida coast. Well, those days are long gone.

When the Japanese bubble burst property prices plummeted more than 80%. It undermined company balance sheets, wiped out massive amounts of personal wealth and helped plunge the Japanese economy into nearly two decades of stagnation. Even though the worst is still to come, I don't believe that we're in for as big a real estate crash as they saw in Japan because our bubble never got as big as theirs. Even so, there's still reason to play it safe and protect yourself from becoming overextended in real estate. If you live in a home, that's one thing but if you're playing the leverage game, watch out because we still haven't hit bottom yet.

If you've been following the news on Japan as I have, you might have a queasy feeling in your stomach about our future as well. We've only had a few years of falling real estate prices in the US, and over much of the world – however Japan has felt the effects of a deleveraging economy for 20 years. That's right! Falling real estate prices throughout most of Japan for two decades! Do you think people in the US, Canada, Europe, Australia or Norway, for example, are prepared for this possibility? Nope. I don't think so either. This is why we've always taught that real estate is a liability rather than an asset, because as you can see from all of this writing on the wall, that's the hard reality of the situation. Simply put, an asset is something that brings in income, and a liability is something that costs you money on an ongoing basis. Sure, investment properties still make sense – assuming you know what you are doing – unfortunately most do not.

I first broke the news that the government was floating the idea of massive interest and principal reductions (forgiveness) on underwater mortgages about two weeks before the news hit the main stream media. If you think the Ground Zero Mosque or even ObamaCare is a bust with the public (or at least the 50% of the public that actually pays taxes), then you might be surprised to find out that a whopping 82% of those polled (according to *Zogby*) believe that principal forgiveness is a terrible idea. Here's why. If your neighbor is underwater on their home and the appraised value is recalculated by the government, guess what happens to the value of your home? That's right – you just witnessed an overnight write-down on your property value as well.

However, since there's no limit to the stupidity that we're witnessing from this administration, don't assume this property value fiasco won't happen. In fact, we should probably be surprised if they DON'T do it. The same geniuses may have another idea in the works in the event of a worst case scenario where the economy continues to decline rapidly (and of course, we know that it is declining rapidly and will continue to do so). Believe it or not, the next idea from their "bankrupt the US as quickly as possible" playbook could be across-the-board credit score increases. Assume that your credit score is 600, which means that you can't buy a home without a down payment of about 30%. The rumored plan could immediately increase your score by 20% to 720, allowing you to buy a home for as little as 5-10% down, or maybe less.

We don't have the time or space here to go over all the problems I have with this idea. Suffice to say, it would cause a massive drop in the value of the US dollar overnight, along with a complete loss of confidence in the US economy globally. In turn, this would cause real estate prices to drop across the board, negating any supposed benefit from this ridiculous idea. Correspondingly we'd see a 20% increase in the value of gold and silver, which of course I would not complain about at all (but we're headed there anyway). Just when you think you've heard it all – now let's see how long it takes for our rain men in DC to officially float these ideas. This much is certain; when the next leg down in real estate begins, look for (at minimum) another taxpayer funded stimulus program for real estate. Just as I'm certain that the FED will launch QEIII to bail out bankrupt states and municipalities, I'm equally certain that we haven't seen the last of the real estate bailouts. In the short term these programs will appear to have worked – but the long-term economic implosion that follows will tell a much more depressing story.

The bottom line here is that there will not be a recovery in the economy until there is a recovery in housing. The shadow inventory (which had totaled 11 million homes) just got dramatically bigger with the additional problems of "fraudclosure" where massive criminal activity by the banks and mortgage servicers is threatening to undermine the very foundation of housing and the mortgage industry. The so-called "experts" disagree on what the "shadow inventory" includes or whether it exists at all. For our purposes here, the shadow inventory is VERY real and includes properties as diverse as "real estate owned" (REO) by banks, high rise condominiums in development, sellers waiting for a better market and foreclosures in process.

The shadow inventory must also take into account the homeowners who have stopped paying on their notes but have yet to hear from the banks – sometimes going as long as 24 months without a foreclosure notice. That's right, millions of homeowners are going 24 months without a mortgage payment and still living in their homes, payment free and responsibility free. For you and me, the significant point to remember here is that together, all of these properties create huge distortions in the "new home inventory" numbers we see in government reports, and therefore in the official story on the true health of the housing market. So, what if the "fraudclosure" scandal creates a huge additional spike in the shadow inventory? Well, get ready for lots of talk about another big bank bailout, because it's on the way.

I've been researching this developing crisis since the beginning, and I'm certain that it's a much bigger deal than the main stream media, the banks, and the government are letting on right now. Surprise, surprise. Here's the simple diagnosis: if we get to the point where 40% of all homes with mortgages are underwater (and we're at least at 30% now) we will see a tidal wave of homeowners buy into this new "fraudclosure" debate, which is; "prove to me that you own the note (not the mortgage) on my home, and then I will continue to make payments to you."

Folks, if you think that millions of homeowners aren't thinking about "strategic defaults" as a financial/business strategy right now, then you're living the life of an ostrich. And if (or when) the mortgage/housing industry becomes a legal drama fought in courts all over the land, it could make the subprime crisis look tiny by comparison. With the robo-signing controversy in the news, attorneys general from numerous states have already fired their the first warning shots at the largest banks with inquiries into millions of existing foreclosures that may have been anywhere from poorly documented to downright fraudulent.

And check out this statistic from the Federal Reserve: In 1980, US debt as a percentage of Gross Domestic Product was 163%. By 2007, it had risen to 346%. What ended this 27 year party was a correction of the most leveraged asset, the US residence. The bust was accelerated by the complexity of the ways in which the Wall Street "masters of the universe" leveraged all of us from the boom all the way through to the bust. Home prices will now correct to their long term moving averages, or an additional 20-30% from where we are today. In some parts of the United States we may already be close to a bottom, but there's another structural problem that people are forgetting about.

Once prices do begin to bottom and trend higher, a wave of sellers will be waiting — they will think that they finally have a chance to get out from underneath the weight that's been on their back for years — and this wave of selling pressure will be a drain on real estate prices for a decade in many markets. This is the very nature of how bubbles expand and collapse, and real estate will be no different. A good analogy here is the dot-com bubble, which finally burst in 2000 after a classic blow-off phase not all that much different from the Dutch tulip bulb mania of several hundred years ago. Here we are a decade later, and the NASDAQ is still close to 50% off its all time highs. Yet most people believe that real estate prices always come back — another old paradigm belief system gone wrong. To fully understand why the stakes are so incredibly high and how this problem has become bloated to its present level, we have to zoom out from the housing crisis to look at the surrounding economic conditions. The implications of this are incredibly serious for all of us.

In a recent article, John Williams (arguably one of the best trackers of real, un-manipulated government data via his *ShadowStats* blog) warned his clients that hyperinflation may hit in less than a year. With so many established economists and pundits seeing nothing but deflation as far as the eye can see, and the FED doing all in its power to prevent any kind of natural deleveraging cycle, how can Williams make a prediction like this with a straight face? I can't quote the entire article here, but I do feel it's important to give you a general idea of his outlook because he and I are on exactly the same page.

He starts out with a pop culture tribute to Aerosmith, saying that the FED is "tap dancing on a land mine." When Wile E. Coyote does it in the Roadrunner cartoons, it's hilarious — when Ben Bernanke does it in front of congress, not so much. So, whether you find that image comical or horrifying (and I'll grimly admit that it's a little of both), it's a pretty accurate description of attempts by the government and the FED to hold off a complete systemic collapse over the past few years. Obviously as business activity keeps spiraling downward, we'll need more and bigger artificial life support measures to keep the system afloat.

The problem is that these actions will also trigger a massive worldwide flight from the dollar and force the FED to buy even more unwanted US Treasury debt with your tax dollars and freshly printed fiat paper. No other country in their right mind is going to want to buy them, so we can kiss the Chinese goodbye as the buyer of last resort. Williams continues the analogy by saying that when that land mine inevitably explodes, all the prerequisites will be in place for the onset of hyperinflation in the US, followed by severe economic, social and political consequences for all of us. To survive and thrive through this period, there are a number of pillars supporting Williams' argument that everyone needs to be aware of.

First, what was already the longest and deepest economic downturn in the US economy since World War II is now getting worse, with zero near-term stability or recovery on the horizon. After a big initial leg down, most key economic indicators I track have been parked near historic lows for more than year. Except for a couple of weak artificial "economic stimulus" spikes there has been no recovery and this has now triggered new contractions in the economy. The main stream media has been happily buying into the "recovery-at-hand" story, calling these new contractions a possible "double dip" but the real statistics don't lie. The underlying reality is that we're experiencing the consequences of one long, deep, continuous downturn across the board.

The second pillar is that a lack of real consumer income growth (made worse by a credit-driven erosion of consumer liquidity) pushed our economy into a recession at least a full year before the "official" onset of December 2007 as reported by the government. These factors helped to trigger the credit collapse, which in turn made the recession worse and brought us to the brink of systemic meltdown. In spite of all of the extraordinary and reckless government efforts to keep our entire banking system from imploding under its own weight, NONE of them addressed the underlying consumer liquidity issues. Until this problem is dealt with head on we will never see any kind of sustainable growth in US business activity. Again, the natural deleveraging process must be allowed to complete itself.

The third pillar is the continuing decline of the US dollar and its gradual elimination as the world's reserve currency. Bailout measures implemented by the government and the FED have pushed our major foreign creditors to the brink of abandoning the dollar and dumping their dollar-denominated assets. As I predicted in the VRA, we've already seen an increasing selloff of the dollar, combined with the FED's ongoing monetization of Treasury debt to boost inflation. As I'm writing this, the signs are clear that these trends are certain to continue until they trigger runaway hyperinflation in the US no later than three years from now. Consider this very carefully – any official forecasts you may have seen on the federal budget deficit, US Treasury funding needs, banking industry solvency stress tests and the like, have all been predicated on some form of economic recovery. Please pay very close attention to this next statement – *there is and will be no recovery for the foreseeable future!* When this reality finally emerges from behind all the smoke and mirrors (and it will very soon), we'll see a massive dumping of the US dollar and near overnight funding problems for the US Treasury, leaving the Federal Reserve in the position as *lender of last resort* to cover the crushing load of our aggregated national debts.

You've heard me say time and again that one of the major reasons this problem is so severe, and has lasted so long, is because our government policies have not allowed our economy to complete a natural deleveraging process. This is the same reason that the Great Depression lasted until World War II started, and would have continued well into the 1950s without WWII. And we've seen this playbook in use recently as well. Under the veiled threat of economic collapse during the 1987 stock market crash, then-Federal Reserve Chairman Alan Greenspan cooked up a plan to forestall an eventual day-of-reckoning for the economy. He did this through massive debt expansion, building financial institutions with leverage on top of leverage. As the financial system started to falter in 2001 and then again in 2007, Greenspan's superficial supports began to fall apart once more. With the end justifying the means, the government and the FED did everything in their collective power to avoid a complete functional failure of the US government and the Federal Reserve System. The disturbing part of this is that all the money they've thrown at symptoms has done nothing to address any of the underlying causes — namely that 40 to 1 leverage can never be a good thing.

Where is all this leading? All we have to do is watch the outcomes of the same policies in other nations to see what's coming here at home. Greece's debt implosion in 2010 was the first canary in the coalmine. History will show that this marked the beginning of the end for the Euro, and was the equivalent of the Bear Stearns blow-up we saw here in the states back in the spring of 2008, just prior to the big financial meltdown in September 2008. Following Greece, Spain's debt was downgraded, resulting in the loss of their AAA status. That marked the beginning of the run on bank deposits in Spain, forcing the European Central Bank (ECB) to follow the FED's US playbook. And it won't stop with Spain, where individuals are closing their bank accounts — this time it will be major banks and investment firms removing hundreds of billions held in just about every European bank. The reason? AAA debt can be held by all, but anything below this guaranteed rating level carries a new degree of risk, and many institutions (such as money market funds and many fixed income portfolios) can ONLY hold AAA rated paper in their investment accounts.

The same playbook they used in Greece will follow throughout Europe; a mass exodus of investment capital and then the panic that brought on the $1 trillion bailout of Greece and the EU just months ago. If it hasn't happened already by the time you read this, they'll use the same playbook in Italy, Portugal, France, Ireland and every other bankrupt European economy. This of course includes the UK. These will be followed by Japan and the US. It's just that big. The only question is timing. You can be sure that we'll hear more promises of global support from the politicians and central bankers, followed by more bailouts into the trillions.

Maybe you couldn't care less about what's happening 5000 miles away. For some, my updates and warnings over the last year or so about Greece may have seemed boring and insignificant. But what if I told you that it would be *your* tax dollars going overseas to bail out Greece, Portugal, Spain, and ultimately the entire Eurozone as well? I probably have your attention now, because that's exactly what's happening. Whether you live in the United States, Canada, Norway, Australia, or any other country that supports the International Monetary Fund (IMF), you just contributed billions to the bailout of Greece. They should really call this deal "Fleece" because markets around the world quickly woke up to the fact that not only was the initial bailout not enough, but also that the European Union (EU) had just used up all of the borrowing capacity that they had to prop up a single country with just 11 million people in it.

Here's the only fact you need to remember when it comes to the problems in Greece. After the bailout was announced, interest rates on two year Greek debt dropped from 14% to under 10%. This was a somewhat encouraging sign that the bailout might just work to restore confidence among the many lenders they needed to continue funding this tiny, but economically important and insolvent country. So, where were the rates on that same two year debt just 24 hours later? *Back to 14% plus!* And here's why – it didn't take long for people to figure out that this incredibly huge sum of money was only enough to paper over the problem in Greece *for 12 months!* The EU was hoping that the bailout would work a miracle, but instead, they once again have to deal with pawn-shop like interest rates – and on short term government debt no less!

This is why I've been saying that Greece is the canary in the coal mine. Again, it's the European version of the Bear Stearns implosion we experienced here in the states, as well as the subprime lending crisis that triggered the worst global economic collapse since the 1930s. And this is ultimately why bailouts never work. Sure, lots of supposedly smart people think that the worst is behind us and we keep hearing hints about a "recovery" in the main stream media that never seems to materialize. Soon, we'll see what their answer will be to the domino-style implosion of the Euro, and along with it, the next stage of the Greatest Depression. Before all of this is over, we'll see the Dow Jones far below 5000.

Let's adjust our zoom lens once again. As you may recall, we were talking about why the crisis in the housing market is so big and so significant. As we've established time after time in these pages, everything's connected. If you're serious about regaining control of your own financial destiny and creating true *Crashproof Prosperity*, you've got to get a grip on the idea that economic events around the world can have a direct bearing on what we experience locally and vice versa. Money is fundamentally a pool of *energy* and we're all in it together, just as President John F. Kennedy observed in his historic American University commencement address when he wisely pointed out that *"...we all breathe the same air."* Just like the Stephen R. Covey quote I mentioned earlier, we're free to choose our actions, but we're not always free to choose the consequences, or who will suffer them.

Bringing our focus back a little closer to home, it's the same faulty "logic" behind international bailouts that should give you serious reservations about the "official" economic statistics reported by your government and the main stream media — especially when they have to do with recovery in the job and housing markets. Here's an example; if you've been wondering how it's possible for the unemployment picture to improve while everything else points to a deepening recession, this will help to clear things up. Art Cashin is a seasoned market analyst who is rarely wrong and his recent insights on government payroll data are revealing.

While everyone's attention was on the headlines from Greece (or the latest drama on *Jersey Shore*) the government's non-farm payroll numbers were barely noticed. The weekend talk show pundits at the time were saying that "we've turned the corner" based on a supposed "jump" of 290,000 new jobs. Cashin's longtime readers (and mine) know that we consider such reports to be suspect at best. For at least two months before those numbers came out, new unemployment claims were averaging about 450,000 per week. That translates to about 1.8 million more people laid off, so how does that pencil out with a claim that 290.000 new jobs were created? Well, the short answer is that it doesn't. Remember what I said in an earlier chapter? Figures don't lie, but liars can figure. Cashin goes on to suggest that we look deeper into the payroll numbers for ourselves to see what's really going on.

The national Bureau of Labor Statistics (BLS) has created a model called the Current Employment Statistics (CES) Birth/ Death adjustment. In this case the terms birth and death do not refer to actual people, but to the survival rate of businesses. The BLS guesses how many new companies opened for business and how many closed their doors. Based on that imaginary number, the BLS then makes another guess as to how many jobs these hypothetical companies may have created or lost. This is where 188,000 of those purported "new jobs" came from.

Another 66,000 "jobs" came from temporary workers hired for the 2010 census — all of whom must eventually be laid off when the census winds down. Another 26,000 were non-census or seasonal temporary workers. So if we add them up, it's now clear that at least 280,000 out of 290,000 "new jobs" had nothing to do with real people getting back to real full time work, or some other sustainable arrangement that a reasonable person would equate with full employment. Also, please recall that as of this writing the real unemployment rate, the important U-6 statistic, is still over 17% and climbing. Does that sound like we've turned a worthwhile "corner" to you?

While we're on the subject of cooked books and rosy predictions, I've received lots of reader feedback about my VRA posts on the consequences of ObamaCare and the inevitable hyperinflation that's on its way for the US (and global) economy. One of the most interesting emails I received was from the UK. This line summed it up best: *"our healthcare system is pathetic, and soon, yours will be too."* I also heard from entrepreneurs and business owners with serious concerns about the ability of their companies to continue providing employee healthcare benefits. And of course this is just what the Obama administration hopes will happen. You see, once a critical mass of employers begin cancelling insurance for their employees, the red carpet will have been rolled out for one of big government's major objectives; the complete nationalization of our healthcare system. My best guess is that we're less than three years away from this eventuality, barring a complete reversal in Congress between now and 2012.

The truth is, with over $100 trillion in total debt and entitlement programs, hyperinflation and the total bankruptcy of the United States of America was already guaranteed. ObamaCare is simply going to speed up the process, but if we're able to reverse it, we would at least send a powerful message to creditors like China, Japan, and the Middle East that the US is serious about shoring up the financial disaster on our national balance sheet. Again, keeping in mind our main point of focusing on reality instead of fantasy, let's take a look at a couple of government programs and their real cost versus the initial estimates we were given.

Medicare was created in 1966 at a cost of $3 billion per year. At the time, official government estimates said that the cost of Medicare in 1990 would reach just $12 billion per year. In 1990 the actual cost of Medicare was $107 billion (792% more than projected). Today, Medicare costs $408 billion annually. In 2003, the government estimated that the Iraq War would have a total cost of $50 to $60 billion. Just so far, we've already spent $713 billion on the Iraq War (over 1,000% more than projected).

Now let's flash forward to ObamaCare. The Congressional Budget Office is estimating that the healthcare bill will cost $940 billion over the next 10 years, but if history is any indication, the actual cost will likely be at least $3 trillion. The National Inflation Association reported that they believe *"the healthcare bill will be the final nail in the coffin of the U.S. economy and will just about guarantee that we will see hyperinflation by the year 2015."*

To put all of this into chilling perspective, we're now at a point where if the US government taxed Americans 100% of their income, the tax receipts generated would not be enough to balance the budget. If you really want a shock, try this one on for size; if the government cut 100% of its spending including defense, but kept paying Social Security, Medicare and Medicaid, we would *still* have a budget deficit. It is now 99% probable that the US will never have a balanced budget again, insuring hyperinflation and the bankruptcy of the USA.

Do you need more proof? Currently, the US is paying about 2.5% interest on all of its outstanding debt. In light of the crisis that the Federal Reserve helped to create, they've kept the Fed Funds rate near 0%, which has allowed the remaining major domestic banks to book big profits and pay out near-record bonuses to the same people who helped to cause this crisis. In 2014, using official government statistics, we'll be looking at a national debt of over $18.5 trillion. And remember, this figure does not include ObamaCare or our entitlement programs. On this $18.5 trillion, it is beyond ridiculous that the government is projecting that the interest rate on this debt in 2014 will only be 4%.

Remember, as our creditors recognize the gravity of these issues and stop buying our government debt, it follows that interest rates *must* begin to rise sharply. It's an economic certainty that this will take place, otherwise, our creditors will simply take their money elsewhere. Add to this a core level of inflation that's already greater than 5% per year when you add food and energy back into the Consumer Price Index (which is the only accurate way that the CPI should be measured). This *real* inflation rate demands interest rates of at least 7% today versus the 0% we currently have. Now, can you imagine where we will be when the reality of all of this hits home and interest rates hit 10% plus?

In 2014, with a 10% interest rate on $18.5 trillion in government debt, total interest payments will equal $1.8 trillion. With total tax revenues of just over $2 trillion, there will be *no* money available for *any* government programs. Nothing for defense, nothing for Medicare, nothing for Medicaid, nothing for Social Security, nothing for social programs, and (you guessed it) nothing for ObamaCare. Can you say *social unrest?*

I began warning my readers about these issues through the VRA back in 2003. Through WMI we've worked hard to prepare our members for the current crisis since 2005. Unfortunately, this is only the third inning of what will eventually become unmanageable. This is a global financial crisis of a magnitude never before seen, and the passing of ObamaCare will only prove that we learned nothing from the lessons of the 1930s.

As it becomes more and more clear that the US economy is incapable of bouncing back on its own, watch for additional stimulus programs to be announced. And the exact scenario I described earlier will play out around the globe. So, don't be surprised to see these idiotic decisions by the powers that be to move stock markets higher in the short term. In fact, this is one of the reasons that our markets continue to rise today, in anticipation of just this sort of action. These moves are already being made in Japan, which announced its own one trillion (yen) stimulus program this year.

And who knows, these massive bailout programs may propel stock markets higher in the months to come. Following the 1929 crash, the government launched one bailout after another until many were convinced that the worst was behind us, only to see the stock market drop nearly 90% in the years to come. In Japan they've repeated just about every page from our 1930s playbook only to see their stock market drop from 38,000 to 8,000 over a 10 year period. This has pushed their debt to levels that make it clear it can never be repaid. And once Japan begins to default, which will begin to happen as soon as interest rates begin to rise again, a domino effect will be set in motion around the world with such speed and force that it's going to be breathtaking in its magnitude.

Folks, regardless of what your realtors and mortgage brokers are telling you, rising interest rates are on their way and they can't be stopped. Hyperinflation is a word that few know or understand, but in the years to come it will become a household name, and it will bring a level of fear and panic that make the last couple of years look tame in comparison. This is the central plot line for the $50 trillion wealth transfer. The greatest transfer of wealth in history is already underway, so make sure you're prepared. With crisis comes opportunity, and in this case it's a once in a multi-century opportunity.

I exercise a lot of self restraint when it comes to making political comments in the VRA newsletter, although it will surprise no one to learn that I'm a fiscal conservative. That generally means I have little in common with the Democratic Party's push for more government in our lives. The line *"trust me, I'm from the government and I'm here to help"* comes to mind again. But to be fair and honest, I'm no fan of the great majority of Republicans either. Politically, I tend to land near my good friend Wayne Allyn Root, the 2008 Libertarian vice presidential nominee and one of the most integrity-driven voices of true fiscal conservatism in America today.

Regardless of which party it comes from, I disagree with any policy that increases our debt beyond the $100 trillion we already owe. We simply owe our children a better future. This obscene level of indebtedness comes from Republicans just as much as Democrats, including the decision to invade and occupy Iraq and Afghanistan (following the governments "official version" of the events of 9/11), and the bailout of 2008, which saw us throw trillions in free money to the very same companies that caused the financial crisis in the first place.

Remember, the stock market always reacts to *anticipated* happenings six months from now, rather than to what's happening today. Using that time frame as a guide, we'll be staring the next leg down in both employment and housing right in the face. There are at least ten million more homes that must still go into foreclosure and unemployment is going to spike sharply as most states run out of taxpayer bailout money, leading to budget cuts and layoffs on a Great Depression-like scale. This when the Obama administration and FED will likely try to pass another massive round of bailouts, but with the utter failure of his first effort, I predict that this second attempt may never get off of the ground, leaving the FED to launch QEIII; effectively forced to deal with future bailouts on their own.

People often ask me how the stock market can continue rising against all the negative news we keep hearing? This is the most difficult thing for investors to get their brains wrapped around. Stocks seem to go up when they should be going down, and vice versa. It's the same with the overall market. Right now the market is "climbing a wall of worry" and this may go on for a while. Global governments are hell-bent on re-inflating the economy and that means that lots of cheap money is being printed and then entering the market. All of that cheap money is looking for a home, but at best it will be just a vacation home rather than permanent residence.

CDs and bonds are paying very little in interest, so they offer little competition to the stock market. This is the government's big plan. Their big bet is that they can bring the economy back from the brink by manipulating the markets higher. Right now it "appears" to be working, but all they're doing is creating a different kind of bubble. This bubble — massive government debt and trillions in freshly printed paper dollars — must inevitably end in the mother of all bear markets. Again, the key thing to watch is interest rates. Once they begin rising rapidly (and they're already up 40% from last year), then you will begin to see panic set in with the powers that be. Remember the late 1970s? We saw interest rates at 20%, inflation at 15% and an unemployment rate of 14%. Now, imagine this same scenario with our current level of debt.

My longtime subscribers know that I preach the importance of individual stock selection. The market can be falling apart but as long as you own solid companies your investments will perform extremely well over the long run. Another way of putting it is that it's a *market of stocks,* not a *stock market.* Having said that, it's incredibly important to have a clear view of the macro environment — how the overall economy is doing (both in the US and globally is doing and how it's expected to do in the months to come. Long term, I'm very concerned about the health of both the US and global economies. Sure, China has held up incredibly well, but outside of this still communist country and maybe Brazil and Australia, there aren't many bright spots to be found around the world. And, once you dig a little deeper into China you will discover that if it were not for their massive government stimulus programs (which were more than twice as large as the US taxpayer funded bailouts), China would be in a serious recession as well.

Of course, commodity rich countries, like Brazil, Canada, Australia, etc., have done well and for obvious reasons; the stuff they're able to extract from the ground has given them lots of valuable exports and reciprocal income. The truth is, if it weren't for China and their decision to provide an artificial foundation for the weakest global economy since the 1930s, we would likely be witnessing a natural bottoming out process today. Instead, we have to endure another decade of deleveraging and pain.

As we enter 2011 the question remains; what happens when the "funny money" runs out? After all, at some point governments around the world will be unable to continue printing and passing out money to replace the spending that consumers are responsible for. And we know that consumers are still spending very little money – that's what happens when people don't have jobs. In the US, over 70% of our economy is driven by consumerism – the stuff that we buy. Globally, these percentages vary from as low as 40% to our high levels domestically.

Now let's return to how all of this is related to the housing market. We now have millions of Americans in the poor house (literally), overloaded with bills, not enough cash flow and just about zero money for discretionary purposes, and heaven forbid any emergencies. Lots of twenty-somethings with overpriced college degrees, young kids in the house or on the way, three or four new leased cars and living McMansion lifestyles are only one paycheck away from financial oblivion. We're talking about dual income families earning $200,000 to $250,000 who are financially broke and emotionally over-burdened.

As the perfect storm of a slowing economy, job layoffs and job reductions arrived, these former "hot stuff" consumers lay in bill-paying wreckage. These folks along with many others are significantly underestimating the future fallout from currency inflation that will end in hyperinflation, and an economic depression of never before seen magnitude. There is no wealth effect remaining – the days of using our homes as ATMs are over. The money is gone, the bills will go unpaid and consumer cash flow has diminished, or stopped entirely.

Look, I know you have to have somewhere to live, but apart from that I still encourage everyone I know to use judgment and caution when it comes to real estate. If you follow our recommendations and watch the market carefully, the time will come in the very near future when you'll be in a position to pick up some amazing bargains, but we're not quite there yet. If you do choose to include investment properties as part of your portfolio, do not buy on impulse and make sure that your holdings are not over leveraged with excessive debt. Once more, contrary to conventional wisdom, real estate is a liability, not an asset.

The FED is doing everything possible to make stock prices rise – which *could* bring back the real estate market – which *could* bring back lending. But it's a losing battle, just as Japan has discovered over the last 20 years. All they have left to show for interventionist strategies like these is a mountain of debt that's mathematically impossible to pay off. Is it becoming clear to you now that we're repeating all of their failed policies all over again? Do we really expect the outcome to be any different? This is why we're so passionate about life-changing products and services like the ones available through Wealth Masters International and the VRA. Every day we help regular people to live the life they have always dreamed about by taking informed action. This is OUR economic stimulus program.

CHAPTER NINE
READER QUESTIONS
FROM WMI AND
VRA MEMBERS

About half way through the process of writing this book, I decided to ask our friends in the Wealth Masters International community to submit their questions and the response was overwhelming with more than 100 questions submitted for review. In reading through them, it became clear to me that people around the world share similar concerns about the future, and a common desire to prepare for what's next. I believe that many of the questions are addressed throughout this book, but I've selected four of them to answer directly. Thanks to everyone that took the time to write to me. All of the questions were great, but the ones I've reprinted for you here are representative of the majority of responses and address what I believe may be our most pressing issues right now.

QUESTION ONE

"Kip, due to radical government spending policies around the world, what do you think is a likely scenario in the years ahead; inflation or deflation? Or even hyperinflation?"

– Per Gunnar Hoem

Per Gunnar is one of WMI's pioneer consultants in Europe, and a close friend as well, so some reading this might think this is a softball question for me to simply knock out of the park. But that's not the case at all. Per Gunnar and I have met on both sides of the ocean over the last year or so and actively debated and discussed this very question. In fact, this is one issue that I see debated more often than almost any other today – the stakes are just that important.

Because the United States is following the exact economic playbook from both the Great Depression and the current lost TWO decades in Japan, it makes a lot of sense to see what effect these policies have had on those economies. And in Japan today, as well as during the Great Depression of the 1930s, both periods saw "deflation" as the end result. Deflation occurs when an extended period of slow to negative Gross Domestic Product results in a lack of economic productivity and a corresponding sharp reduction in demand for bank lending. It's a pretty simple economic equation; a weak economy = lack of demand = decreased need for bank borrowing = lower prices on almost all products and services. This is the definition and end result of deflation, with most Keynesian economists viewing it as the one economic condition that must be avoided (too bad they don't understand that the natural deleveraging process must eventually run its course).

And, while all of these events are happening right now throughout the US, Europe, and Japan, there is one major difference – and I believe that this one factor will result in not just inflation, but hyperinflation. And that difference is the massive printing of all fiat currencies, which is exactly what we're experiencing today. You see, the financial leaders of our bankrupt countries have made the decision to issue as much debt as possible and to print as much funny money as possible in order to re-inflate banks' balance sheets, which should in theory re-inflate our moribund economies. But it's not working too well is it? And instead of restoring a growing economy, we're printing and issuing our way to total bankruptcy.

Soon, we'll reach a tipping point where our creditors no longer see us as trustworthy – simply not a good credit risk – which will leave us exactly where Weimer Germany was in the 1920s. At this point we'll be forced to print increasingly huge amounts of fiat money just to buy our own debt; in fact this is exactly what the FED is doing right now through the massive Ponzi scheme we covered earlier called Quantitative Easing. We've actually reached QE II now, which will see the FED purchase another $2 trillion or so of our own government and toxic mortgage debt in the coming 12-18 months. This is of course on top of the $2 trillion in debt that the FED has already purchased. These Ponzi schemes on steroids guarantee a world of currency inflation – which will soon go out of control with fiat currency printing and hyperinflation. Or put another way, a FED led lab experiment into financial engineering of this magnitude will create a Frankenstein of unimaginable proportions. And the naïve villagers — citizens of each country — will pay the ultimate price.

QUESTION TWO

"Kip, how can so many so-called experts and advisors all have such different opinions about our economy — and whom do we ultimately believe?"

— Fran Kennedy

Great question Fran, and it's one that more and more people are asking every day. By the way, I think that's a very good thing. For generations we trusted most of the "experts" in our lives to have our best interests at heart. We trusted our doctors, our lawyers, our CPAs and our financial advisors, among others — pretty much implicitly for a very long time — but that's changed big time, and seemingly overnight. The reason? The technology age has morphed into the information age and information is now our most valuable commodity. Unfortunately (or very fortunately), we're being forced to learn that no one cares more about our money, our health, and our future than we do. And while this means that we must work to find our own sources to trust, the good news is that in doing so we learn the truth in the process. I'm more than just a little biased, but this is exactly why I started publishing the VRA and why Karl and I founded WMI — to be that trusted source offering the best of the best in wealth, health and wisdom.

QUESTION THREE

"Kip, I am a Member of WMI and I get all of your messages and am blessed to have you share your vision with me and the rest of the world. I shudder to think what lies ahead for the young adults of the world. So, as an aunt – who absolutely believes in preparing for tough times to come – what would you say to the parents of such young adults to get them to at least consider following your advice and helping children NOW to do something about their financial situations?"

— Lisa Smith

Thanks Lisa. Your question was actually more involved than the part that I've included here and I know that this has been a bit of a family struggle for you. And you are not alone. At our WMI Conferences, we sometimes show a picture of an ostrich with its head stuck in the sand because sadly, this represents a large percentage of the population. But think about it this way; in most cases we were all raised with just about the worst financial planners possible – our parents. Of course it's not that our parents intentionally gave us bad advice about financial planning, or purposely withheld the truth about how money works – they simply didn't have this acquired knowledge themselves. And again, in most cases their parents didn't either.

Our leadership and our education system has failed us —
bottom line — so it's up to us to learn the truth about the old
paradigm versus the new paradigm, and to then pass this on to
our kids — or in your case your nieces and nephews. We are leaving
this next generation a financial and moral mess to clean up, but
I don't have a doubt that they will be up to the challenge. A good
place to start is by giving them a copy of *The Conspiracy Against
Your Money*, WMI's documentary that explains the real world
"matrix" that we live in. And getting them started with a gift of
either the m^{POWER} Program or even the full m^1 Masters Program
is a great idea as well. My two boys were much more advanced
—aka street smart — than I was at their age (in some good ways
and some bad ways), and because they understood the principals
of money and capitalism since they were about 10, I'm sure your
nieces and nephews will as well.

Another great idea is to gift them with copies of the Rhino
Books by Scott Alexander, a good friend to WMI for years. This
trilogy is written at about the third grade level and emphasizes
the difference between the cow and the rhino in nature. Rhinos
"charge!" through life while cows "graze" through life, and in
adulthood we each become one or the other. It's a choice, regardless
of what anyone (or your nieces or nephews) may tell you. These
books explain independent thinking and competitive, free market
capitalism as well as anything I've read — well, except maybe for
Think and Grow Rich by Napoleon Hill, which is required reading
for anyone and everyone that desires wealth and freedom. Lisa,
I think you may have some new stocking stuffers for Christmas.

QUESTION FOUR

"Kip, how can I best prepare myself to act on these multigenerational opportunities? I am retired and still have a lot of good years in me to accomplish much. How can I make the most of these years to leave a legacy for my children?"

— Sallie Brown

Sallie, this question is perhaps the most important of all. And it's something that everyone reading this book thinks about on a daily basis — if not a legacy for your children then for other pressing financial concerns and goals. As I have traveled and spoken around the world over the last couple of years I am finding that people everywhere are genuinely fearful for their futures. More and more often they're asking things like "will I still have an opportunity to live the life of my dreams," and more importantly, "will my children have the ability to have a better life than I have?"

So, while I'm seeing more fear out there than I have at any other point in my life, you are asking the right question, which is "how do I not only survive but prosper greatly from it?" And while I've done my best to answer this question throughout this book, let me try and sum it up for you here as concisely as possible. I believe that we are at the precipice of major changes globally. Most developed countries are in fact bankrupt, and the situation is even more dire when it comes to the state of individual households. In the near term (and by that I mean the next three years or so), those that prepare for the coming economic implosion will be positioned to buy "real assets" at dirt cheap, multi-generationally low prices.

You know that I'm a big believer in real currencies (gold and silver) and that I also believe that those heavily leveraged to the US dollar (and most all fiat currencies globally), along with leveraged exposure to real estate and government and municipal debt will be the big losers. In addition, those that follow their entrepreneurial calling and create their own wealth, instead of making someone else rich, will be way ahead of the game. And of course those that follow the education we offer and adopt the principals of the new paradigm will be positioned perfectly when we reach a true economic bottom — which as I see as three to five years from now. The economic realities that await will be a tough pill for lots of us to take, but it's the only outcome that makes sense to me as a free market believer.

CHAPTER TEN
EVENT HORIZON

For decades, folks have been fascinated by the astrophysics breakthroughs of Stephen Hawking, particularly in the field of black holes, where all known laws of the universe seem to unravel into mystery. From a university chair once occupied by Isaac Newton, Hawking's popular books and documentaries have done so much to make science accessible to everyday people that his iconic "computer voice" has even been parodied on *The Simpsons*. Hawking has theorized that black holes contain the most densely packed matter in the universe, resulting from the cataclysmic finale of collapsed stars. Our own galaxy is believed to be revolving around one right now as part of a cosmic cycle that's been playing out for billions of years.

Because of their mind-boggling density, it's believed that nothing – not even light – can escape the gravitational pull of a black hole. Once any object passes a boundary called the "event horizon" near the edge of a black hole, it will be pulled inexorably inward toward the same unknown oblivion that awaited the hapless Homer Simpson. Why am I telling you all this? Besides all the amazing things they can teach us about the origins of the universe, black holes happen to be a perfect illustration of the irresistible forces at work right here on our own planet. You see, you and I are also crossing an economic "event horizon" – an invisible point of no return – beyond which the gravitational pull of massive debt and currency debasement will produce inescapable consequences. For some, it will mean financial doom. For others, it will bring wealth creation opportunities that only come along once in several lifetimes.

It's my belief that all of the financial fraud and moral decay in our top levels of government and business may be happening in advance of some "external event." Everywhere I go people seem to instinctively feel that something is wrong, and I believe they're right. Every time I'm on stage, wherever in the world that might be, I ask the same question; *"How many of you believe that something major is upside down in the world, and even if you can't put your finger on exactly what that 'thing' might be, instinctively you feel it to your core?"* The show of hands in the audience is consistently over 90%, which I truly find overwhelming and more than a little scary. It remains to be seen what all of this is leading. One possibility is that under the new fiscally conservative leadership that emerged in the last round of midterm elections, the FED will finally be audited and we'll learn the whole truth about their massive criminality.

Apart from big revelations about our government and financial institutions, there's been broad speculation about these kinds of history-making events on a much larger scale. With the Mayan calendar set to end in 2012, it's likely that fear will be prevalent, just as it was with the Y2K scare before the clocks rolled over to the year 2000. Some predict another major terrorist event more devastating than the 9/11 attacks. More controversial observers go as far as to suggest that long secret government evidence may emerge that "we're not alone," as unimpeachable retired military sources recently revealed from personal experience, under oath before congress and the National Press Club (if you doubt this last statement, simply Google "Air Force UFO Claims").

It's not my intent to get into a "science versus superstition" debate. The point I'm making here is that to whatever degree and in whatever form, our assumptions about the world around us are going to be challenged – even shaken – in a very big way. The point of *Crashproof Prosperity* is not to run off to a mountain cave and become some kind of prophecy nut – it's to become a critical thinker who focuses in a disciplined and objective way on PREPARATION. Furthermore, my purpose here is to get you to take action based on how things *really* are – not based on how you *wish* they were. That's partly how the old paradigm lulled us all into the mess we're in now. The old paradigm is dead, never to return. Having said all that, my Wall Street experience and my passion for relentless research are showing me some important trends and I'd like to give you my "most likely" interpretation of the indicators as I see them today.

I'm not trying to be a fear monger — not the kind of fear that overwhelms and paralyzes people, anyway. Like I said before, if I scare you at all, I want to scare you into *action*. I'm writing this because I want you to be as prepared as you can possibly be for what's coming, and the *only* way to do that is to take informed action. The following views are my personal opinions on what I see happening. Confidence in the old paradigm has been lost. What we've seen so far is just the beginning, and it truly makes me sad to have to write this. Most people have no clue about what's really going on, and since Karl and I founded WMI in January of 2005, we've done our absolute best to make sure that people like you are educated and ready for these possibilities.

The biggest certainty I see on the "event horizon" is massive hyperinflation, thanks to the disastrous policies of the FED and their partners in crime from other central banks around the globe. The onset of this financial meltdown is going to be sudden and breathtaking, and the consequences here in the US will rival the shocking stories we heard about Weimar Germany and, more recently, Zimbabwe. Citizens in these imploded economies carried millions (or more!) in virtually worthless paper currency around in wheelbarrows simply for daily necessities like a loaf of bread and it won't be long before we see it happen on the same scale, or worse, right here at home.

Need more convincing on how bad things can get in this kind of currency crisis? Harvard law Professor Friedrich Kessler was quoted in a 1933 interview as saying *"It was horrible. Horrible! Like lightning it struck. No one was prepared. You cannot imagine the rapidity with which the whole thing happened. The shelves in the grocery stores were empty. You could buy nothing with your paper money."* Why should we trust what Kessler said? Because he personally lived through the crisis.

Want a more recent, first hand example of a crisis brought on by fiat currency? The following is from good friend and WMI Member John Arnold. *"In early 1991 I was invited into the USSR to do some mountain climbing. It was during the country's debt and currency crisis and just after the Soviet army killed 13 students protesting for freedom at the TV Tower in Vilnius Lithuania. Things were tense while staying in Vilnius and at night we would hear loud booms over head...the Russian helicopters flying low to intimidate the people. The ruble was nearly worthless and we had to smuggle in US Dollars hidden under the insoles of our double climbing boots so that we could buy basic necessities. I remember looking into department stores in downtown Moscow and seeing nothing on the shelves. Seeing people lined up around the block to buy potatoes and cabbage and having to trade in their gold jewelry to do so. It is one thing to read about it or see it on TV, but it's a very different thing to experience. It has always stayed with me".*

In his groundbreaking *Trends Journal*, Gerald Celente (not a man who indulges in exaggeration or hysterics), is forecasting social unrest right here in the United States similar to what we've seen around the world as banks and governments continue to fail. Here's how things will most likely play out in the next few years. Expect the real unemployment rate (based on true

U-6 figures, remember) to rise above 25%. You, or several family members and people that you care deeply for, will lose a job. Home prices will continue to fall for the next three years , and in some areas will plummet anywhere from 30% to 50%, and quite possibly even more, from 2010 levels. All over the world, large and small banks will continue to fail and "bank runs" will become a common occurrence. The value of the US dollar will also fall sharply, causing massive inflation that will evolve into hyperinflation. Stock prices may continue to rise during the early stages of inflation, but that will change radically, just as we saw in the fourth quarter of 2008. At minimum, we'll experience a "near depression" that will feel like a serious Depression for most. If you're in the middle class, you'll likely slide into poverty unless you begin to take action now.

But while most people will suffer, you have an opportunity to prosper because you've taken the steps to begin educating yourself on the new paradigm. A massive number of new millionaires will be made during this very painful period as millions of others sadly become homeless. This is it. This is a time that will go down in history, and this is why we created Wealth Masters and the VRA, so that you can have a fighting chance to join the informed few who know how to position themselves for these events and profit from them.

Everywhere I go, people tell me they're hopeful that the worst of the crisis is over, but I can tell that instinctively they don't believe that's really the case. Unfortunately, their instincts are going to be proven right. In the coming year, I'll be writing a lot about the following trends, because recognizing and understanding them will be the only way to hold on to any kind of personal and financial solvency. Now is the time to be decisive. You can't afford to sit on the sidelines and there will be no "do-overs." You'll most likely be wiped out unless you take control of your financial destiny, but as always, the choice is yours.

Here's an important observation that few are aware of. Did you know that in the US and the Eurozone (the 16 member states in Europe that use the Euro), anywhere from 40% to 80% of all government bond purchases are currently being made *by their own central banks?* That's right, the Federal Reserve (US) and the European Central Bank (ECB) are responsible for as much as 80% of all government bond buys. If this sounds strange to you, well, that's because it is. And if you're guessing that the real reason is that *no one else will buy this debt* at artificially low interest rates (due to the inherent credit risks) then you're absolutely right. Would you loan money to someone that's bankrupt and has no mathematical possibility of paying you back? Well, you might, because you're a good and decent person, but if you're reasonably intelligent, you certainly wouldn't expect to ever get that money back!

But don't take my word as gospel. Current Federal Reserve board member Thomas Hoenig was quoted recently as saying that *"Bernanke has made a deal with the devil"* and that Quantitative Easing or QE (the Fed's ongoing bond purchase program) is a *"dangerous program that is creating too 'bigger' to fail."* Hoenig also warned back in 1999 that repealing the 1933 Glass-Steagall

Act would come back to haunt us, which turned out to be one of the most prescient statements by any government leader – certainly better than the incredibly pathetic forecasts of Greenspan and Bernanke over the last decade. If we had kept Glass-Steagall, then we would never have had "too big to fail" because the Bear Stearns, AIGs, Lehman Brothers, JP Morgans, and Citigroups of the world would never have existed in the first place.

But what does this mean for you and me, both in the US as well as globally? After all, the ECB and Bank of Japan are acting just as aggressively as the FED in buying every government bond in sight. On the surface it might appear as if both QEI and QEII (which will total over $2 trillion in bond buys when all is said and done) are working. After all, global stock markets are going up and unemployment isn't skyrocketing – not yet at least. But here's the flaw in that argument. You see, without the unprecedented level of financial manipulation by the FED and ECB, interest rates would be skyrocketing upward at a frightening rate, just as they did in Greece and Ireland before the ECB stepped in and became the buyer of last resort.

And here's the really important point; the kind of rate increase I'm talking about is the way a free market system *should* operate. Trust me, the run up in interest rates is exactly what *will* happen when the FED and ECB run out of bullets (that is, when they run out of credibility). That's when the currency crisis will really kick into high gear and that's what hyperinflation is all about. It will go something like this:

Step1: Interest rates will begin to rise as the inherent credit risk in government bonds leads countries like China to not only suspend their buying, but to actually begin selling their bond holdings. Oh wait — this is happening NOW! Of course, this is only the beginning of the huge increase in interest rates. Yes, even central banks have limits to the amount of government bonds they can buy.

Step 2: After the bond vigilantes really begin doing their thing (see step 1), the public will begin to fear a repeat of the late 1970s and early 1980s — and for good reason. In case you've forgotten, this was when interest rates hit 20%, with inflation topping 15%. If this idea is new to you, don't worry — economists are second only to sports junkies for falling in love with their own arcane jargon. In simplistic terms, a "bond vigilante" is a bond market investor who protests inflationary monetary policies by selling bonds to drive up yields.

Step 3: Real estate will see its next big collapse. Studies show that every 1% move higher in mortgage interest rates triggers a corresponding 5% (on average) drop in real estate prices. That means that if mortgage rates go back to just 8%, real estate prices could fall another 18%. And if mortgage rates go back to 12%, we could be looking at a 35% collapse, even from today's already weak housing market.

Step 4: The stock market – let me just say that it will look quite a bit different than it does today. Rising interest rates are never a good thing for stock prices, but skyrocketing interest rates cause nothing short of a collapse. This is why I get so frustrated when I hear "old paradigm" Wall Street types continue to tell people to buy mutual funds. Hey, if you're a great market timer you *might* be able to make a little more money in the stock market before the final top is in place. I just don't know many people who are very good at that game. Besides that, there are just so many better places to put your money! The *big* winners will continue to be gold and silver and some of the unique wealth creation strategies built around them.

You see, through their actions, central banks all over the world are telling us – no, they're screaming at us – that they intend to print as much money and issue as much debt as possible in the months and years to come. This is the biggest invitation that investors will ever get to buy gold and silver. The best advice I can give you now is to continue to follow your instincts and to work only with those who really know what they're doing. In times like these, plenty of charlatans come out of the woodwork, ready and willing to take your hard earned money.

Check writing in the trillions is not a bondholder's friend; it is in fact inflationary, and if truth be told, it's somewhat of a

Ponzi scheme. Public debt, actually, has always had a Ponzi-like characteristic. Granted, the US has at times managed to pay down its national debt, but it was always assumed that as long as creditors could be found to roll over existing loans – and buy new ones – the game could keep going on forever. Sovereign countries have always implicitly acknowledged that the existing debt would never be paid off because they would "grow" their way out of the predicament, allowing future prosperity to continually pay for consumption in the present. When you strip away all the Ivy League business school lingo, Wimpy's character in the vintage *Popeye* cartoons expressed their whole theory in one line when he said *"I'll gladly pay you Tuesday for a hamburger TODAY!"*

Now, however, with any kind of growth in serious doubt, it seems that the FED has taken Charles Ponzi one step further. The FED, in effect, is telling the markets not to worry about our fiscal deficits; it will be the buyer of first and perhaps last resort. There is no need as with Charles Ponzi to find an increasing amount of future gullibles – they'll just write the checks themselves. Has there ever been a Ponzi scheme so brazen? There has not. This one is so unique that it deserves a new name. I call it a "Sammy" scheme in honor of Uncle Sam and the politicians (and yes, the citizens) who have brought us to this critical moment in time. To be completely fair, it's not a Bernanke scheme because it's his only alternative and he shares only some of the responsibility for its origin. Truly, the blame rests squarely on you, me and the politicians we elect every two to four years.

Okay, I have no idea how many times I've actually written about the subject of unintended consequences over the years, but I do know this; it's been a common theme of my research for a long while. When manipulation, fraud and insider dealing take place, especially at the levels we're witnessing today, history tells us that there will be an equal amount of unintended consequences to be dealt with somewhere down the road. It's that whole karma thing — it finds a way of kicking you in the butt when you least expect it. I don't want to get carried away with too many numbered lists, but my forecasts about the size and scope of unintended consequences we'll be forced to deal with in the months ahead includes the following:

1) With more than $100 trillion in U.S. government debt and entitlement program promises, what happens when (not if) long term interest rates simply double from 4% to 8%? We've already seen it happen this year in Greece, Hungary, Portugal and Ireland, with Spain (to name just a few) right behind them. How will the United States continue to fund even our base level commitments as long-term interest rates double, and then some?

2) Same scenario, but Japan this time. Japan's debt-to-GDP ratio is 200% more than double the already ludicrous rate in the US. Currently, close to 50% of all Japanese tax revenues must be used simply to pay the interest on their debt. And they must also raise $2.5 trillion over the next year just to replace the debt that's maturing over that same time frame, because they obviously can't afford to

pay it off. Add to this Japan's rapidly deteriorating demographics, where families are having fewer and fewer children due to the overall financial condition of the country, and we run into the same question again. How will Japan continue to fund even *their* base level commitments when long-term interest rates double, and then some?

3) Ben Bernanke (it's so much more fun to call him "Bernocchio") stated on the CBS weekly news program *60 Minutes* that he was "100% certain" that he could contain inflation. My response was that I don't think I can be 100% certain about anything. But Ben, have you not seen the amount of inflation we're witnessing right now? Take a look at the level of inflation we're seeing in oil, gold, silver, copper, wheat, meat, and cotton (just to name a few). The average inflation rate of these goods is in excess of 40% in just the last six months! And Bernanke calls that "containing" inflation?

Folks, this is exactly what I've been warning about. The massive level of dollar printing going on today (due entirely to the FED's Quantitative Easing and trillions in fraudulent bailouts) is having the biggest impact on those who can least afford it. This list includes the 45 million Americans on food stamps and the one in five households that currently receive government assistance. Exactly how are they supposed to see an economic recovery in their lives (let alone anything within sniffing distance of prosperity) when they can't even afford to buy groceries or pay their electric bills? Talk about unintended consequences! But of course the bankers, Wall Street con men and highly paid government workers at the federal and state level will be fine – the same people who caused this crisis, no less! Obviously we need to remind our so-called leaders that we're only as strong as our weakest link. And this is a global issue as much (if not more so) than it is for us here in the US.

4) Let's also give some consideration to the unintended consequence of fraud, deception and the widespread erosion of citizens' trust in their governments. *WikiLeaks* and Julian Assange are great examples of this type of unintended consequence – or as Sir Walter Scott put it *"Oh what a tangled web we weave, when first we practice to deceive."* Governments around the world – maybe for the first time ever – are under siege for their attempts to grab an unprecedented level of power and control. Instead, the only outcome may be a string of multi-national bankruptcies, and in the process, a multi-generational loss of faith in political leaders of any kind. This may be the ultimate unintended consequence that changes everything forever.

I'm not the only one making these predictions. If you validate these sources for yourself, you'll find that lot of trustworthy independent thinkers are drawing the same conclusions from the same indicators. While I was attending the world's foremost anti-aging conference in Las Vegas recently, I had dinner with political/media legend and rising Libertarian Party luminary Wayne Allyn Root. Wayne is a dear friend and it's always interesting spending time with him and picking his brain. Wayne's instincts and timing are as good as anyone I know, and I asked him about his forecast for 2011. It was simply this; *"2011 will be the year that the Depression really begins."* Thanks, Wayne — great talking with you. We hope you're wrong, but we'll be prepared either way. Unfortunately, I don't think he's wrong.

One by one, insiders from the Federal Reserve System are beginning to "break ranks" and distance themselves from Ben Bernanke. Although their public statements are still veiled and very carefully worded, the situation brings back a very vivid memory of what happened to former FED Chairman Paul Volcker back in 1987. I recently saw an opinion piece on this subject by John Tamny in *Forbes* that really grabbed my attention in a big way. He quoted FED Governor Ken Warsh's indirect slam on the Chairman less than a week after Ben Bernanke spelled out his justification for more Quantitative Easing in the *Washington Post.*

Hollering right back from the editorial pages of the *Wall Street Journal*, Warsh's statements revealed a lot about policy conflicts inside the FED. Although Warsh had voted in favor of Bernanke's plan, the tactic reminded me a lot of the playbook Volcker's detractors used in 1987. I couldn't help thinking that as a FED Governor, Warsh wouldn't have been so outspoken in the *Journal* unless he knew in advance that others on the board were going to back him up. Richmond's FED President Jeffrey Lacker and Kansas City's FED President Thomas Hoenig (mentioned earlier) have both publicly criticized Bernanke's bungled economic stimulus efforts. All of this suggests to me that Warsh thought his own op-ed piece through very carefully and made certain that he had significant support behind him before it went to print.

In the same thought-provoking *Forbes* article, Tamny raises another key point we should all pay close attention to. If the discontent over QE being voiced by top economic figures outside the FED is any indication of the buzz going on inside the FED itself, Bernanke could end up with a serious palace revolt on his hands. Looking back at how Volcker's exit played out during the Reagan era, it seems that the writing is pretty much on the wall for Bernanke's future at the helm of the world's most powerful central bank.

Could this be part of the back story behind the recent rise in Treasury yields? Are the markets starting to "price in" an impending reversal of Bernanke's failed Quantitative Easing policies? Even though the results would only be temporary, it wouldn't hurt the stock market if Bernanke finally walked away from a job that's clearly beyond his reach. But with nothing more than guesswork to go on for now, investors are going to stay cautious until they know for sure how things are going to play out at the FED. It looks like Bernanke is not only losing control of the system, but also losing credibility with former allies on the FED board just the way we saw it happen to Volcker.

The hubris in Bernanke's claim of 100% certainty that he can control inflation is breathtaking. The US economy is a complex interaction of thousands of variables and it's intertwined with the policies and actions of hundreds of other countries throughout the world. No one has a handle on the worldwide economy and no model can predict anything with any amount of accuracy. And still, this pompous professor from Princeton who has never worked a day in his life in the real world is 100% certain that he knows what will happen and when it will happen. Just in case you think his critics are being unfair, let's examine again some of his earlier pronouncements;

July 1st, 2005 – "We've never had a decline in house prices on a nationwide basis. So, what I think what is more likely is that house prices will slow, maybe stabilize, might slow consumption spending a bit. I don't think it's going to drive the economy too far from its full employment path, though."

February 15th, 2006 – "Housing markets are cooling a bit. Our expectation is that the decline in activity or the slowing in activity will be moderate, that house prices will probably continue to rise."

March 28th, 2007 – "At this juncture the impact on the broader economy and financial markets of the problems in the subprime markets seems likely to be contained,"

May 17th, 2007 – "While rising delinquencies and foreclosures will continue to weigh heavily on the housing market this year, it will not cripple the U.S."

June 20th, 2007 – "[the subprime fallout] will not affect the economy overall."

October 15th, 2007 – "It is not the responsibility of the Federal Reserve – nor would it be appropriate – to protect lenders and investors from the consequences of their financial decisions."

February 29th, 2008 – "I expect there will be some failures. I don't anticipate any serious problems of that sort among the large internationally active banks that make up a very substantial part of our banking system."

June 9th, 2008 – "Despite a recent spike in the nation's unemployment rate, the danger that the economy has fallen into a substantial downturn appears to have waned."

July 16th, 2008 – "[Freddie and Fannie] will make it through the storm...in no danger of failing...adequately capitalized."

September 19th, 2008 – "...most severe financial crisis in the post-World War II era...investment banks are seeing tremendous runs on their cash...without action, they will fail soon."

As you've already seen in these pages, I've had a lot of fun over the years with nicknames for Bernanke (Helicopter Ben, Bernocchio), but here's the bottom line. I mentioned earlier that history may not repeat itself, but it certainly rhymes. The reality is that Bernanke is considered a laughingstock by those who truly understand money. If I had to call it based on what I see today, my forecast is that Bernanke will go down as a cautionary tale against the dangers of hiring academics for jobs that should be held by those that have actually done them in the real world. I won't be surprised to see a Washington-style press conference in the very near future announcing that Bernanke is quietly "retiring" with whatever face he can manage to save.

Where is all of this taking us? In a recent TV interview, leading trends forecaster and futurist Gerald Celente discussed unemployment among college grads, the wide income gap between the rich and the poor in the US, and the fact that the events in Greece are headed our way. *"You have millions of college grads that haven't entered the workforce yet that haven't been able to get jobs out of college and they have degrees in worthlessness, and they're $25,000 on average in debt."*

Celente goes on to predict that the collapse to come in US cities will rival what's going on in Ireland right now and what's about to happen in Portugal. *"The American Empire is unfolding and collapsing in front of everyone's eyes,"* he says. Celente's proposed solution includes bringing production jobs back to the US, shutting down military bases around the world, ending the wars, and cutting massive overseas spending. You can find his complete interviews on this and other topics on *YouTube* and at his web site, *TrendsJournal.com.*

I've been warning my readers for a long time now about the truth this entire chapter has been pointing to — that the next big economic crash will be the direct result of one very large unintended consequence. The good news is that we *may* have a window of time to prepare — a window to help those that we care about locally and globally — to help ensure that they're not among the newly bankrupt, morally, spiritually and of course financially. Over the years I've done my absolute best to research these very issues – to make sure that those I impact with my work are given the most solid advice possible.

After all the advice is weighed on its merits, achieving true *Crashproof Prosperity* is ultimately about self determination. It eventually comes down to each one of us to decide for ourselves the course of action we're going to take as individuals. Will we choose to invest in precious metals over old paradigm assets that are in fact nothing more than liabilities? Will we do the tough internal work necessary to learn to think like a contrarian, knowing that the mainstream majority is almost always wrong? And, will we learn to focus on the real definition of abundance – a prosperity mindset based in the universal principal of abundance we explored in the introduction to this book – *"what you think about you bring about."* It's never about the destination. It's the journey that makes everything we do so incredibly worthwhile.

CHAPTER ELEVEN
THE UNIVERSAL LAW
OF ABUNDANCE

Things that used to be simple have now become complicated. What's worked for most of us for our entire lives (if not for generations) isn't working anymore. As we've seen in the previous chapters, the economy and the job market aren't what they used to be, the stock and real estate markets have imploded and government "fixes" just don't seem to be helping us now (if they ever did). Folks find themselves struggling harder and harder to hold on to comforts they once took for granted. They may have trouble putting it into words, but more and more people are voicing a vague, foreboding sense that for the average person, the system is broken. Most people don't respond to change all that well even in the best of times, and now many are being forced to change in big new ways that make them even more uncomfortable.

Those who understand what true abundance is all about know that moments of great discomfort often mean that great opportunity is nearby – for the few who recognize the signs and act on them. If that's true, then why is it that we tend to associate great losses with times of great adversity? It's a fair question. Sadly, it's because the vast majority of people attach a false sense of security to feeling comfortable. The primitive parts of our brains are biologically wired to retreat in times of trouble, even though we no longer face any of the real physical threats that were part of everyday life for our ancestors. When they did manage to outrun that saber-toothed tiger, they didn't just cower in their caves (or a therapist's office) waiting for the next predator to wander by – they shook it off and went right back to the business of living.

In modern times, the ones who consistently survive and thrive no matter what may be happening around them have trained themselves to overcome that "retreat" programming and ACT in the face of fear. They know that anything worth having (and keeping) is just outside of their comfort zone. In fact, those who know me will often hear me say that your *comfort zone* is your *failure zone* – to get anywhere worth going in life, you've got to learn to reach beyond it to what I call your *achievement zone.* Today, the majority are so overwhelmed and paralyzed by fear that they're unable to see or respond to the opportunities for positive change that are literally all around them. Confusion and fear keep us trapped in our comfort zones indefinitely while incredible opportunities pass us by.

I've heard two versions of this story and I'm not sure which one's true, but either way, it's a powerful illustration of the confusion and complacency that keep people trapped in a perpetual state of lack. The lighter version involves lab monkeys who reach into a specially designed jar for treats, only to find that the opening is barely big enough for their empty hands to pass through. Most will sit there indefinitely with a fistful of goodies they can't enjoy, unable to pull their little hands out yet unwilling to let go of the perceived reward. The darker version describes non-lethal cages of a similar design that are baited by South American hunters or poachers. The monkeys stubbornly cling to the bait, totally unaware that certain captivity or death is creeping up behind them. I can't imagine a more vivid and horrifying illustration of the price each of us pays for clinging to our comfort zones. Folks, I'm going to say this as plainly and honestly as I can — there's no need for us to live this way any longer.

Years from now, when people look back on the once-in-a-lifetime economic environment we're in today, *new paradigm* adopters will realize that they made significant changes for the better. It's an inescapable fact that major lifestyle changes are going to happen. The only question is whether folks will make them by their own free will or by force. Wouldn't you rather be in the group that ends up better off? My hope is that everyone reading this book will take advantage of this economic environment and break free from the insidious trap of the *comfort zone.* Only when you make the decision to leap into the *achievement zone* will you begin to enjoy life to the fullest possible extent.

But how do you DO that? That's the true secret to *Crashproof Prosperity* and that's what this chapter is all about. A growing number of entrepreneurs, like the WMI Consultants I work with every day, approach *every* opportunity with this mindset and I want you to learn how to do it too. Real people just like you (with no greater internal or external advantages than you already possess right now) are achieving the kind of financial success that places them in the top 1% worldwide. Their financial concerns are a thing of the past – forever – but the mental, physical and spiritual skills that enabled them to do this won't be found in stock charts, economic theories or banking histories.

I could easily fill another whole book with these ideas, but to make the point in a way that will enable you to start acting on it today, I've asked three great friends who have actually mastered this way of thinking to tell you how they did it. First you'll hear some powerful country wisdom from Karl Bessey, my "brother from another mother" and WMI Co-Founder. Next up, Deanna Latson, health expert extraordinaire and one of WMI's best friends, will share the amazing and unbreakable link between wealth and wellness. Finally, Wayne Allyn Root, one of America's last trustworthy media voices and one of our best political hopes for the future, will teach you what can happen in your life when you stand up and decide to be relentless.

Each one of these individuals has faced adversities as real as any you may have encountered in life and overcome them in their own way. Each one offers their own unique perspective on how you can achieve prosperity as you define it and on your own terms – just like they did. These are more than just theories or good ideas – they're the time-tested habits that countless self-made millionaires have used throughout the centuries to create not just massive generational wealth, but true and lasting abundance in every area of their lives. That's what living in the new paradigm *achievement zone* will do for you and I want you to start living there too.

KARL BESSEY

Have you ever wondered why some people are so successful and others are not? Stop and look around. We all know people in our community or old classmates from high school that have gone on to hit it big. So what makes them different from others? What do they possess that we don't? What does it truly take to be an entrepreneur and develop that mindset of success? And is it something we're born with or can anyone acquire it? As I considered these questions for myself over the years, it made me wonder how and where I first became addicted to the idea of one day having my own business. I want to turn the clock back to the sixties when I was a young boy growing up in the world surrounded by successful entrepreneurs.

As I mentioned in *Two Roads, One Journey* with Kip Herriage, my first taste of entrepreneurship was hanging out with my Grandfather at his full service Conoco gas station. Seeing him interact with people and the way the customers who came in respected him was such a cool experience for me that I couldn't imagine being anywhere else or doing business any other way. As I watched and learned, I saw him develop loyal customers one by one who came and went time and time again all through my childhood and teenage years. I came to know them all on a first name basis. It was a great learning experience to see him in action, but I really had no idea at the time that the seed had been planted for me to one day be in business for myself.

I actually got a double dose of being an entrepreneur because like my Grandfather, my Mother and Father started out with a Dairy Queen location early in their marriage and eventually ended up in the restaurant business. I did work there on and off for a bit as well, but preferred getting my hands dirty working alongside my Grandfather at the service station. Wherever he was, I wanted to be there too, doing what he was doing.

Jumping ahead a few years, I married soon after graduating from High school and then got a job in the underground coal mines in Central Utah. Fifteen years later those early seeds of entrepreneurship began to sprout. I started to experiment and tried a few different business ventures that were mostly unsuccessful. The point is that I had been infected with the dreamer's disease early in my life as I witnessed the autonomy and flexibility my Grandfather and my Dad had by operating their own businesses. I was ready and primed for a piece of that action — but little did I know at this point the challenges I was going to face by having a business of my own. That was something I began to understand gradually through the school of hard knocks.

I got involved in the direct sales arena in 1999, finally fired my boss and ended a 22 year career as an underground coal miner in August of that year. It was the scariest thing I had ever done in my life. No longer could I count on the steady paycheck that I was in the habit of picking up at the post office every two weeks like clockwork. My income was now totally dependent on the actions I took and no one else's. If you've ever done this you know exactly what I'm talking about. There was no emergency slush fund set aside for a rainy day. All I had was credit cards, and for some reason they kept allowing me to increase my limits until they were maxed out to the tune of about $36,000.

In the beginning, it was a struggle for me to change my mindset and quit thinking about all the debt, but I realized it would take a lot more than a great work ethic to get my financial life on track. So, I began to follow the teaching of many successful people that I respected and admired. To summarize what I learned from them, I'll cover what I think are the most important success habits and ways of thinking used by the world's most successful entrepreneurs and how you can learn to make them a part of your own life, just like I did.

The very first step is to take an honest look at how you really feel about yourself. Not what you think you're *supposed* to feel, but your honest core belief about who you really are. Do you see yourself as someone who deserves to acquire all the happiness, material and spiritual possession that are waiting for you? If you don't feel good about who you are or feel comfortable in your own skin, then this is the first place to start. Remember this – it's going to be pretty much impossible for you to achieve any kind of lasting wealth if deep down inside you don't truly believe that you deserve to have it. Be honest with yourself as you analyze YOU. The only one you're cheating here is yourself and nobody else. So where do we start building (or re-building) this kind of belief system?

1. Read and listen to powerful positive self improvement information and cut negativity out of your life completely.

2. Have a regular routine each day for exercise both mental and physical.

3. Develop healthy eating habits and treat your body with care and respect.

4. Clearly visualize what you want to attract or accomplish in your life each day.

5. Surround yourself with people who have the qualities you want to have.

6. Start and finish each day by giving thanks for all that you have.

Immersing yourself in powerful positive self improvement information is the quickest way to get from where you are to where you want to be. Your mind is the most complex computer in existence and if you constantly have good information going in, then good things will pour out. When I say cut negativity out of your life, I don't just mean avoiding negative people or gossip, although that's important too. I mean turn off the TV. Quit listening to the news and main stream media. Learn something new each day instead of being brain dead in front of the tube. Read something uplifting each morning before starting your day and each night before lights out until the success thoughts and habits of an entrepreneur are ingrained in your daily life.

A regular workout is essential for peak performance both mentally and physically. Make sure you have a daily exercise routine for your body and stick to it. It doesn't matter what it is, as long as it gets you moving every day, even if it's only for ten or fifteen minutes when you first start out. I personally don't like gyms or weights, but love a ride on my mountain bike, shooting hoops on my basketball court or backpacking in the mountains. It can be yoga or a gym for you but make sure you do it consistently several times a week. Proper rest is also an important part of total fitness. I'm big on what I call "power naps" and try to set aside 30 to 40 minutes each day to turn the world off and meditate and rest. In most cases I don't fall asleep, but I'll still relax and cleanse my mind for half an hour. You'll be amazed how this can energize you.

I know Deanna is going to cover this in detail, but I have to put in my own two cents here and stress how important good eating habits are for overall physical and mental health. If you're not getting the nutrients your body needs for peak performance then how can you expect to operate at 110%? Years ago, I used to have a 1965 Corvette coupe – the one with the Chevy 427 big block. That sucker ran about a thirteen second quarter mile – pretty good for a street car. But if just one spark plug began to miss or the points began to corrode it instantly went from a smooth ride to a sputter and pop. It's the same with the marvelous human machine we all pack around with us. Eat great home cooked food regularly and you'll feel the difference.

I learned early in my entrepreneurial career that what you *think* about you *bring* about. Clearly visualizing what you want to attract or accomplish in your life keeps you focused on what's truly important each day. The minute you make an important decision in your life, especially one that involves positive change, you can count on someone trying to talk you out of it – events are going to get in your way. Without a clear picture of what you want, why you want it and where you're going, there's no way your commitment can withstand all the distractions and temptations that bombard us day and night. So take time every day to close your eyes and visualize what you want in life. Do this during the power nap or meditation time you set aside each day.

Experts say that in a very short time, your life (not to mention your bank account) is going to be a reflection of the five people you spend the most time with. Surround yourself with people who are living the way you want to live. Successful people don't surround themselves with folks who lead mediocre lives – they hang out with positive people who inspire and motivate them. They choose mentors they can learn from – not the negative folks with a lifetime membership in the "ain't it awful" club. Which kind of person are you? Successful people have problems just like the rest of us, but what sets them apart is that they've developed a habit of focusing on the *solutions* instead. All their energy is directed toward success and yours will be too if you spend your time with the people who make it a habit to think this way.

I mentioned gratitude as number six on my list of success habits, but in reality, gratitude comes first. If you truly want to achieve lasting success in life, make it an unbreakable habit to start and finish each day by giving thanks for all that you have. I believe in the power of the universe and I've seen from firsthand experience that the universe responds to gratitude. I know that if I put good things out, good things will show up in my life. I make it a point each day to give thanks for all I have been given — especially my family, my friends and my business associates, from whom I get so much love and support. I'm thankful for my home, my health and the food, clothing and experiences I'm so blessed to enjoy. So whether it's in meditation, a list, a journal or just conversation with a trusted friend, make sure to give thanks each day in whatever fashion you choose and I promise you that the results will be powerful.

These are the steps I followed, and I'm convinced beyond a doubt that if you apply them consistently, they'll work for you too. For me, being an entrepreneur has been the most gratifying and rewarding experience on earth. It takes drive, determination and desire to turn your life around from the mundane days of working hard and making someone else richer. It feels magical for entrepreneurs when things fall into place and success seems to find us each and every day. We're inspired by thinking of our business and ways to improve it 24 hours a day. We love to spring out of bed early to get to work and then look at the clock 10 or 12 hours later wondering where the time went. When you're living your right life and doing what you love, you lose track of time because you're so focused and having so much fun every hour or the day.

Your life will change dramatically when you too become a true entrepreneur. Although most self-made millionaires share this same simple list of success habits, every success story is different. Everyone begins from where they are and some may have to work harder than others to develop the mindset, the skills and work habits to be a successful entrepreneur. I don't remember saying it would be easy, but what I can guarantee you is that it will be worth it.

WAYNE ALLYN ROOT

Relentless is what separates the men from the boys. *Relentless* is that special ingredient that allows a "nobody" to become a "somebody." *Relentless* empowers anyone with a big enough heart to overcome insurmountable odds; to smash though barriers; to break glass ceilings; to surmount adversity, challenge and fear; to make the impossible POSSIBLE. When I speak across the globe on the topic of success, my presentations are always called RELENTLESS. There are many factors integral to achieving success – but none are more important than simply being relentless. Never giving up. Never giving in. Never accepting the word impossible. As Winston Churchill (one of my heroes) once said in the darkest hours of World War II, Never, never, never, ever give up or give in. If you are relentless, ANYTHING is possible.

I'm often asked, "How do you stay positive in the face of failure, challenge, adversity, even tragedy? How do you keep the faith in the face of long or impossible odds? It's one thing to say 'be relentless,' but how do you keep the faith, when no one else sees what you see, Wayne?" The answer is simple: Get Passionate. Take action. And, BELIEVE! I'm a huge sports fan. One of the great things about sports is that every year people achieve things that no one ever expected, or believed possible.

Examples abound in sports of players and coaches who struggle and lose year after year. Fans may give up on them, but they never give up on themselves. Then, they're signed or hired in the right place at the right time, in the perfect situation for their talents. Suddenly coaches that have been losers their entire careers win the Super Bowl or the World Series. Quarterbacks who have been losers their entire careers make the Hall of Fame. Running backs who couldn't find a hole move to another team and wind up in the Pro Bowl. Career "backups" become stars seemingly overnight with a change of scenery or a new game plan. Teams with a history of pathetic losses win a championship and then go on to create a long-term tradition of excellence.

The Boston Red Sox are a perfect example. For almost a century they were cursed and considered losers – until they won a World Series...and then another. Now they're a dynasty. The curse is forgotten. Few experts believed the hapless Red Sox were capable of this kind of success – until it happened.

Joe Torre was a subpar baseball manager who was fired from three jobs – until he joined the Yankees and became the best manager of his generation. Joe was a miserable 286–420 as manager of the New York Mets. Then he was a mediocre 351–354 as manager of the St. Louis Cardinals. Both stints led to firings. When he was later hired as manager of the New York Yankees, the media and fans rebelled. The New York media called him "Clueless Joe." That was before he led the Yankees to six World

Series appearances and four world championships in 12 glorious seasons as manager. Now Joe is a surefire Hall of Famer. Few experts believed Joe Torre was capable of this kind of success – until it happened.

The New England Patriots were perennial losers until they found the right owner (Robert Kraft), who hired the right head coach (Bill Belichick), who found the right quarterback (Tom Brady). That was four Super Bowl victories ago. Now it's hard to remember a time when the Patriots weren't an NFL dynasty. A few years ago no one believed it was possible – until it happened.

Ironically, Pete Carroll was the New England head coach before Bill Belichick arrived on the scene to build a winning tradition. Carroll failed miserably, fired after only three seasons at the helm of the Patriots. That result was actually better than his record as head coach of the New York Jets, where he was fired after only one miserable season. Carroll's NFL head coaching career was over before it started. Yet soon after, he was hired as head coach of the USC Trojans. The media and fans reacted in outright shock and dismay. The choice appeared so flawed that thousands of USC alumni threatened to withhold donations to the school until Carroll was fired.

That was before he won two national championships, seven consecutive PAC 10 championships, and coached the USC Trojans to seven consecutive 11 win seasons (an all-time college football record). Pete Carroll became the first coach in history to win three consecutive Rose Bowls (and four out of six). Carroll became the winningest active coach in college football. His USC Trojans were voted the "Team of the Decade" by ESPN. He is now considered one of the greatest coaches in college football history and is now back in the NFL as Head Coach of the Seattle Seahawks. Few experts believed Pete Carroll was capable of this kind of success – until it happened.

But the best coaching turnaround in history has got to be the magic act performed by Turner Gill as head coach of the Buffalo Bulls. Never heard of this small college team? Join the club. Most fans didn't even know that Buffalo had a college football team until Turner Gill came along. When Gill arrived in 2005, Buffalo was one of the worst teams in college football. They had won only 10 games over the past seven seasons. But Turner Gill believed. He told the players and press that "UB (University of Buffalo) now stands for "U Believe!" By 2008, Gill's third year as head coach, Buffalo won the MAC championship game, propelling the Bulls to their first bowl game in the football program's 92-year history. He was soon hired by Kansas of the Big 12 Conference to turnaround their storied program. No one ever believes – until it happens.

Of course the U.S. Olympic Hockey team (filled with amateur college players) beating mighty Team Russia (filled with professional champions) counts as THE biggest upset in sports history. As announcer Al Michaels said, "Do you believe in miracles?" Miracles happen every day. Long odds are overcome every day. The impossible becomes possible when RELENTLESS people refuse to give up or give in.

A fact of life is that timing is not important . . . it's everything! Things change in a hurry when the right man (or woman) meets his or her destiny. Mountains can be moved when the pieces of the puzzle fall together, in the right situation, at the right time, in the right place. Suddenly the impossible, becomes possible. It happens virtually every year in sports. That's why our country loves sports – because of the magical, miraculous moments. But before you can move mountains or pull off miracles, first you've got to believe in yourself – and then you've got to be relentless in pursuing your goal.

The impossible and magical happens in politics, too. I'm living proof. I was there at the very beginning of the New York State Conservative Party. I was just a kid, but I clearly remember how futile it all seemed. We were like rebels with pitchforks fighting the powerful British Empire. I remember powerful, wealthy Republican leaders literally snickering at my father and mother. The big shots that ran the New York State GOP were all politically connected – lawyers and power brokers with Ivy League degrees. My dad was just . . . *gasp* . . . a butcher! My mom was the cashier at the butcher store. To the New York crowd we were just a bunch of poor, powerless, amateur nobodies. We must have seemed like Jed Clampett and his family of hillbillies arriving in Beverly Hills (except without the windfall oil money).

The odds were insurmountable that this ragtag third party would ever elect anyone – until 1971 when we elected James Buckley as U.S. Senator in perhaps the biggest political upset ever. From that point on the Conservative Party was known as the kingmaker of New York politics. From that point on Republicans literally begged for our endorsement. Since 1974, no Republican has won a statewide race in the state of New York without Conservative Party endorsement. That means it's been almost 40 years since the big, bad, powerful Republicans won a statewide race without the help of the Conservative Party. Score a big victory for the peasants with the pitchforks. Who would have ever believed that? No one ever believes – until it happens.

It's remarkable how it can all change overnight. But first you've got to believe in yourself . . . and then you've got to be relentless. Let's fast-forward a few years to 2008. I'm sure no one thought a Las Vegas oddsmaker, a complete unknown in political circles, was going to win the Libertarian Party vice presidential nomination either. My odds looked insurmountable. Then things got worse – a former four-term U.S. Congressman (Bob Barr) and former U.S. Senator (Mike Gravel) entered the race. At that point my odds looked downright infinitesimal – so poor, in fact, that the Washington Post actually erased me from a photo of the Libertarian presidential debate. Now that's pretty pathetic. But I never lost faith. I never stopped believing that I would make the "impossible" possible. I kept on being relentless. I almost won the Presidential nomination. Next thing you know, I was standing at the podium with arms raised, accepting the Libertarian Party nomination for Vice President of the United States.

No one who knew my background should have been surprised. Relentless is in my genes. Let me tell you a remarkable, magical, extraordinary story that literally defines relentless – the story of the last hours of my mother, Stella Root's life. My mother and father died of cancer 28 days apart in 1992, the hardest year of my life. I spoke at my father's funeral in New York and returned to my home in California only to get a call a few days later from my sister telling me that our mom had gone into a tailspin after the funeral. Twenty-eight days later she was gone. But it was the remarkable last hours of Stella Root's life that I will remember and cherish forever.

"Wayne, I'm sorry to tell you this, but your mom is gone. Her brain no longer has activity, so we're disconnecting life support. Please don't rush home. She's gone. You've had enough tragedy in your family for one month. You have a new baby on the way that depends on you. So be careful, take care of yourself, breathe deep, and don't rush. Doctor's orders. Got it?" Those were the words I heard from my mother's physician on the last day of her life. Then he handed the phone to my sister, who whispered because she was afraid the doctor would hear what she had to say and she'd sound foolish, *"Wayne . . . rush home. Because you and I both know that mom won't die until you get here. Rush home!"*

I caught the red eye flight that night out of Los Angeles to New York. The flight left late. It taxied on the runway forever. I ordered a car to pick me up at JFK airport to rush me to the hospital in Westchester County. But the car was caught in traffic and arrived late. Everything that *could* go wrong *did.* By the time I walked into my mother's hospital room it had been 12 hours since I got that terrible phone call; 12 hours since life support had been disconnected; 12 hours since that doctor said, *"Don't rush home, your mom is gone."*

Yet when I raced through the door to her room, I heard the most beautiful sound I'd ever heard. *Beep . . . beep . . . beep.* It was her heart monitor beeping. Despite being disconnected from life support, her heart was still beating. My sister had sat by her bedside all night saying, *"Mom, hang on, Wayne is on the way. Don't die, Wayne is on the way."* Medical science may have determined that her brain was dead, but that beeping heart monitor told another story. She'd lived through the night on sheer willpower. Some might call it a miracle. I simply call it relentless.

I hugged my mom and grabbed her hand. I kissed her cheek. I couldn't stop crying. I said, "Mom, I love you. Thank you for waiting for me. I know how hard that was. But I made it . . . and you made it. I'll always remember what you did for me. You showed those doctors. I love you . . . but you've fought cancer for six long years...now it's time to go. You deserve a rest. Heaven is waiting. You can go. I give you permission to let go." And within seconds, her heart monitor went *beep . . . beep (fainter) . . . beeeeeep . . .* flatline. She was gone.

Medical science may have considered her brain dead, but somehow, some way, my mother had understood what was being said. She heard my sister's pleas to hang on all night long. If her brain was dead, how did she know to hang on all night long . . . and into the next morning? How did she know that her son Wayne was on the way? If her brain was dead, how did she hear me say that it was time to let go? Why did her heart monitor stop within seconds of my giving her permission to let go?

My mother may not have had any brainpower left, but she had willpower. She certainly had heart. And that's the most important thing in the world — no matter what your goal. All success, all progress, all the miracles in this world are based on heart, on spirit, on will, on being relentless. My mother was relentless. She beat cancer for six long years, coming back from dead a dozen times. She beat the odds because she had a huge heart. She had spirit and relentless willpower. In those last hours of her life, she refused to lose faith, to give up, to give in — even though medical science had written her off. To the medical experts, she was brain dead.

Stella Root defined relentless her whole life. She wasn't going to die without saying good-bye to her only son, her baby boy Wayne. Stella Root proved that heart is what matters in life. Heart is more important than the diagnosis of experts, or doctors, or scientists, or science itself. Hard facts don't matter when heart is involved. Heart is what makes miracles happen. Heart makes the "impossible" possible. My mom's story proves that if your heart is big enough, it doesn't even matter if your brain is dead.

So when people ask, *"How can you be elected President, Wayne? The Libertarian Party has never achieved any major success — no third party has ever elected a President in modern political history. How will you overcome those impossible odds?"* My answer is "I don't care. That was then. This is now." The Libertarian Party has had fine candidates, smart candidates, even brilliant candidates in the past. The LP certainly has a great message — the right message. But the missing ingredient up until now has been heart. I am Stella Root's son. I am relentless. I have a bigger heart than a thousand candidates. More heart than all the others that came before me – combined. Heart is the missing link – the missing ingredient that has the power to turn the right message into a winning message. Heart is the straw that stirs the drink.

Being smart is a good thing. Being educated is a good thing. Brainpower in a political leader is a good thing. But they are not the most important things. Willpower trumps brainpower. Heart is the intangible that's impossible to replace. Heart is the game-changer. Heart is that special ingredient that brings it all together to win Super Bowl and World Series titles, championship boxing matches – and, yes, to win national political elections. Heart is what determines champions. Heart is the thing that separates life's winners from losers. Heart, as the younger generation might say, is the bomb.

I inherited heart, spirit, will, and a tenacious, passionate, never-say-die attitude from my mother. I am relentless. If I have to, I will drag this party ... like Jack LaLanne celebrating his 70th birthday by dragging 70 rowboats with 70 people through Long Beach Harbor – with his teeth. That's relentless. That's heart. That's what this party, this freedom movement, has been missing. We have had plenty of intellect, plenty of brainpower, plenty of good ideas, but up until now, not enough heart. Without that one ingredient, all the rest is rendered meaningless.

From this day forward, the buck stops here. The Libertarian Party now has a fighter to lead the way – a passionate, committed, tenacious, relentless fighter with the biggest heart in all of politics. It may take 8 years ... or 12 ... or 16 ... or even 20 years. But I'll see you at the White House. And the day I put my hand on that bible, I know one thing for certain – David and Stella Root will be looking down from heaven with the biggest smiles ever and with their hearts bursting with joy. They'll look at their son, shake their heads, and say, "Relentless."

What's your goal? Do others tell you it's impossible? Do you believe? Now's the time to dig down deep. Relentless will get you across the finish line – no matter how long the odds.

DEANNA LATSON

I've learned that most people, most of the time are *reactive* not *proactive* when it comes to life. That is, many of us are not particularly good at taking charge of our own futures – our health, our relationships, our career, our finances, our destiny – in short, our lives. We tend to spend our lives reacting to events, situations and circumstances, rather than creating and shaping them. Do these examples sound familiar? We get sick (and scared), so we make a decision to start an exercise program or eat better to "get healthy" (reactive). Our partner leaves us (we get scared), so we decide to be a better partner and do anything to make it work (reactive).

Living a life based on reactive decisions, made out of fear and limited options, is never going to be the path to your *best* life, but that's what many of us do. Reactive people wait until they are sick and then decide to do something about it. Proactive people understand that great health is a lifelong process and they choose to live their lives keeping their bodies healthy. Sometimes reactive people get lucky and they get the opportunity to turn their lives around. Most of the time it's too late and they've already done permanent damage with no ability to heal the body. By improving the health of your body you can prevent all sorts of illnesses and diseases. Healthy people rarely suffer from colds, flu or even cancer.

If you don't have your *health* today, then you can count on spending a large portion of your *wealth* (and your time) taking care of it later in life. Spending your money and time going to doctors throughout the week will not be the way many people envision spending their retirement years. This will be the harsh reality for reactive people. So many of us are blind to what's going on around us. We take advice from sick-looking doctors, we take nutrition advice from fat people, and we blindly take prescription drugs because a pharmaceutical sales rep says we need it. Wake up! If your doctor doesn't look healthy, run. If a fat person is telling you how to lose weight, walk away. If your doctor gives prescription medications make sure you know the side effects. People who don't practice what they preach have absolutely no place telling you what to do when it comes to your health and well being. Can you imagine going to a Dentist with no teeth?

Great health is your true wealth but it's not a given. It's a balance of physical activity, great food and emotional mastery. There was a time in my life when my health was at great risk, but I've learned to care very much about (and for) my health because of what it provides; great energy, less sick time, enhanced performance, clearer thinking, increased enthusiasm, feelings of well being and better looks. Who said there's anything wrong with looking good?

If you want to start eating better, here's an easy rule of thumb to remember. Anything florescent green, pink, purple, blue or any outrageously bright color is not real food! Think chemicals. A friend Dustin called me one day and I could hear him chewing on the phone. I asked him what he was eating. *"I'm not telling you,"* he said. I begged him to. Finally he gave in and said, *"Okay, I'm eating Girl Scout cookies."* I asked him to read me the first ingredient on the label that he couldn't pronounce. He paused for a minute and said, *"I knew I should never have told you what I was eating!"*

He read the first ingredient that seemed to be in Latin. I quickly looked it up in one of my favorite books, *A Consumer's Dictionary of Food Additives* by Ruth Winter. This book tells you exactly what's in the food you're eating (yes, I'm a nutritional geek). Anyhow, I found the ingredient and read the description to Dustin, *"...known to cause gastrointestinal problems in infants and young children."* Then I said, *"To think that they allow that terrible ingredient in Girl Scout cookies!"* Dustin paused in shock for a minute. Then he proclaimed, *"They just sell the things; they don't have to eat them!"* The point here is that so much of what ails us today (allergies, heartburn, constipation, acne, low energy, cancer, obesity, diabetes and heart attacks) is directly related to how we're taking care of our bodies and what we're putting in our mouths. Read labels on the food you're eating. If you don't know what it is or what's in it, don't eat it. Learn about ingredients so you can make better choices about what you feed your body.

Here's another myth you need to get over if you want to be healthy. Fast food is not food. It may be cheap, tasty, and convenient, but fast food is loaded with saturated fat and calories, and it's low in fiber and nutrients. Thanks in large part to fast food, half of America's adults and a quarter of its children are obese. That's double the rate of a generation ago! Even some popular chicken nuggets, which many people consider a healthier alternative, are flavored with beef extract and contain twice as much fat, ounce for ounce, as a hamburger.

The immediate effects of high fat or sugary snacks can be totally misleading. They might give you a quick burst of energy and may reduce tension. But these effects can start to run in reverse very rapidly. Why? Fast food and junk food are usually the most processed foods, where the nutrients are refined to the point that they're either absorbed immediately or not at all, leaving no long-term substance for the body to feed on. Researchers agree that it can be addictive to eat that sort of lipid-laden diet.

Besides the poor nutrient content, fast food often contains many additives and preservatives that can negatively affect mood. Food colorings, preservatives like benzoates and flavorings like monosodium glutamate (also known as MSG) can cause anxiety. Studies have also shown that the omega 6 fatty acids often found in these foods can compete with omega 3 fatty acids and an imbalance between the two can lead to obesity and depression. Science Americans don't get enough omega 3 fatty acids in their diets, consuming too many fast food items automatically puts you at greater risk for mood disorders.

To better understand your eating habits (because most of us are in denial), the best method I've found is to keep a food diary.

Stop what you're doing right now and go out and get a small pad of paper that fits into your pocket. Now for one entire week write down everything you put in your mouth. Everything. This is by far the best way to understand how much real food you're putting in your mouth. If you're like the average, obedient American consumer, after keeping a daily food log for one week, you'll be shocked to see just how much junk food you're really eating. Junk food is addictive and we must get over those addictions to live a healthy life.

According to scientists at Scripps Research Institute in Jupiter, Florida, junk food alters the brain's chemistry by releasing dopamine that would normally be released when having sex, snorting cocaine or eating a rich dessert. In 2010, Florida researchers gave a group of rats unlimited access to a calorie-laden diet of bacon, pound cake, candy bars and other junk food. Predictably, the rats quickly gained lots of weight. As they plumped up, however, eating became such a compulsion that they kept chowing down even when they knew they would receive an unpleasant electric shock to their feet if they did so.

The most startling part of the was that when they took the junk food away from the obese rats and replaced it with healthier food, the obese rats went on something of a hunger strike. For two weeks, they refused to eat hardly anything at all. *"They went into voluntary starvation,"* said study author Paul Kenny, an associate professor at Scripps. The junk-food-addicted rats learned that the easiest way to experience pleasure was to eat high-calorie, high-fat food. This phenomenon isn't exclusive to rats. I've been a practicing nutritionist long enough to know that humans get just as addicted to junk food as they do to alcohol or drugs. Lesson for the day; there are far less dangerous ways to be a fun parent than to let your kids eat junk food!

Here's a little tip for all the men reading this book. Junk food does not discriminate and every artery in the body can clog when you eat it. Yes EVERY artery. Erectile dysfunction (ED) may be the first sign cardiovascular troubles, say experts. Scientists have discovered that erectile dysfunction may serve as an early warning sign for health problems like angina, heart disease and stroke. It makes sense, doesn't it? If you turn on your kitchen faucet and you don't get any flow, either the faucet is broken or the pipes are clogged.

So are you *Eating to Live*, or *Living to Eat?* What is your own responsibility with regard to your health and well being? Do you think that cancer just happened to you? Do you think that heart disease just happened to you? Or are you taking responsibility for your well-being and paying attention to the ways in which you have abused your body? If you're ready to step up and start taking more responsibility for your health, here are some practical things you can start doing right now:

1. Define healthy for yourself. What does healthy really mean to you?

2. Take an honest look in the mirror and ask yourself if you're living a healthy life.

3. Don't leave everything in the hands of your doctors. They can only do so much.

4. Start that food journal TODAY and fill it in
   faithfully for an entire week.

With regard to doctors, my best advice is to be a bad patient. Yes a BAD one. I'm not saying you have to be rude or mean or anything – just be more invested in your own health care. Do your homework. Dig for information. Get second opinions. Ask lots of questions even if it annoys the doctors. Understand what is happening to YOU. Remember that doctors have been trained to care for sick people, not healthy ones. It's easier to let your doctor take care of you but it's certainly not safer. Individuals who take charge of their own health and well-being are the people who live longer, more productive and more abundant lives.

To put all of this into perspective, here is one of my favorite quotes from a wise old Ayurvedic proverb: *"When diet is wrong medicine is of no use. When diet is correct medicine is of no need."* This is the kind of vibrant, abundant wellness I wish for you and for everyone you care about. If you'll make this commitment to yourself and really stick to it with no excuses, you'll discover as I did that your health truly is your wealth.

KIP HERRIAGE

In their own beautiful, individual voices, Karl, Deanna and Wayne are all saying basically the same thing – there's far more to understanding what true abundance is all about than the deceptive company line you've been fed by politicians, pop culture and the "perps" on Wall Street. Anyone who desires to build real wealth that will last has to discover for themselves that prosperity involves far more than just the amount of money you may have at any particular time in your life. In the preceding chapters we've talked a lot about the different kinds of risks in the world today, from falling markets to rising inflation to outright criminal corruption among the very people and institutions we once looked to for inspiration, help and hope.

People have been conditioned to look at risk as a negative, but the truly wealthy have learned to embrace risk during tough times, not by being reckless, but by being independent thinkers. The 90 % that don't get this are still attempting to live a safe life by following the old broken paradigm; get a good job, live below your means, be a saver and never risk money on investments. Saving money is a losing proposition that guarantees a life of need and want, especially when the "money" we're saving is being printed into oblivion. Remember that fiat currency is losing value each and every year as inflation eats away at our purchasing power. This is why inflation is called the "silent tax."

By taking informed action that others may consider risky, it's possible to put yourself in the top 10% of the world's financial elite. Remember what we established earlier? Your comfort zone is your FAILURE zone. Recall this quote from Gandhi: *"First they ignore you...then they ridicule you...then they fight you...then you win."* Kindergarteners are taught to raise a hand before speaking, to act with the group, and to accept the majority view as the correct (and safe) one. Individual thinking is discouraged, and most decide it's safer to adopt the "go along to get along" mindset.

Those that have the temerity to think outside the box and share those views with others get labeled as eccentric and kooky, if not radical and dangerous. That's what many thought of Gandhi as he taught the people of India to resist tyranny through nonviolent civil disobedience. Though the "majority" believed it was impossible, Gandhi made independence for India a reality by thinking independently. Is it crazy to link the accomplishments of one of the most principled leaders of all time to the concept of wealth creation? OR...is this the exact way we should approach our own "impossible" dreams?

What's dangerous is to seek the acceptance of others instead of thinking independently and then committing to action that supports your true purpose. When you break free from "group think" you'll develop the inner confidence you need to reach new heights. Your independent thinking will likely be ignored and ridiculed at first. When people get uncomfortable and begin to fight you, you'll know that you've won. My experiences on Wall Street taught me that the majority is usually wrong. It's the contrarians throughout history that have created the vast majority of personal success by helping others get what they want. Lemmings don't do too well when they go over that cliff together. It's YOUR life. Why live it to win somebody else's approval (or make somebody else rich)?

One of the most fulfilling parts of my work is the privilege of meeting entrepreneurs, VRA subscribers and Wealth Masters community members all over the world. When we're one-on-one, I often ask them point blank if they're really serious about building great wealth. It's a rhetorical question, but the answers always fascinate me and lead me back to Napoleon Hill's all-time best selling classic *Think and Grow Rich.* Besides being one of the most compelling success stories you'll ever read, it also happens to contain THE secret to building massive wealth in your own life.

Hill's book was the result of painstaking research and interviews involving over 500 of the world's most successful men and women in an effort to discover the *exact method* they used to achieve their goals. Included among these super achievers were Thomas Edison, Henry Ford, Theodore Roosevelt, Charles Schwab, Alexander Graham Bell, John D. Rockefeller, and many other names you'd recognize. What Hill discovered – incredibly, really – was that each of these self-made titans of business shared one identical secret to amassing untold wealth and success in each of their lives.

In the introduction of the book, Hill mentions a *hidden secret* which reveals the exact "how to" methodology of thought and action to achieve the goals you desire – goals that reach far beyond the idea of mere financial success. To quote Hill, *"Throughout this philosophy will be found the suggestion that thought, backed by strong desire, has a tendency to transmute itself into its physical equivalent."* Because I've seen this exact process work its magic in my own life (countless times), and in the lives of so many close friends and business associates, I get goose bumps every time I think about this phrase. The truth is that it's not only possible to transmute thoughts into their physical equivalent, but when done in concert with a white hot burning desire, it's almost impossible *not* to see these miracles take place in your life.

Like any truly great teacher, Napoleon Hill didn't directly state what the hidden secret is in his book, but he did leave several clues for us in the introduction to help each reader discover the secret for themselves. I'm not going to spoil the secret for you either – the journey itself is too important and too much fun. What I will do, however, is give you my all-time favorite Napoleon Hill quote: *"Whatever the mind can conceive and believe, it can achieve."* Remember this – whether you think you can or you can't, you are right! Without stating specifically what the secret is, I will say this; within each of us lie the basic building blocks, tools, and above all else, the potential to become incredibly wealthy.

Hill's book should be required reading in every high school and university the world over. If you don't already own it, I encourage you to buy it today and visit the Napoleon Hill Foundation web site at *www.naphill.org* where you can find out more about Hill's life story and sign up for free newsletters and daily emails. This one book has helped to create more millionaires than all other business books combined!

The unique idea about the acquisition of money is that it doesn't favor one person over another. Think about this statement for a moment. Money is just one more manifestation of that universal energy field we talked about in the introduction to this book. It's nothing more than an esoteric commodity that flows freely to anyone that demands it. The operative word in that sentence is *demands*, because specificity is what gives goals their power. The sad reality is that most people go about setting goals in a way that guarantees that they'll never achieve them.

The majority focus on their past; constantly dwelling either on what they didn't do or on what they did wrong. Then they go about trying to correct those "mistakes" the next time around. By concentrating on the negatives in your life, you virtually ensure you'll repeat those same mistakes, time and time again.

What if you were to focus instead on what you actually want out of life? The more clear and specific you are about your vision, the more likely it is to become a reality in your life, and the sooner it's likely to happen. Think about it this way; your emotions and your thoughts act as a magnet to your reality. As Karl mentioned earlier, whatever you think about, you will most certainly bring about. Growing up without much money taught me a very valuable lesson; I wanted to HAVE money! Sure, having a nice home, nice cars and all the toys is fun, but more valuable than all of those things is the peace of mind that comes from financial success.

As a boy I used to imagine where I'd be and what my life would be like in the 21st Century. Most kids do that and I imagine that you did as well, so let me ask you a question. Does the life you're living today look like you thought it might 10, 20 or 30 years ago? I'd be willing to wager that as you considered that question your thoughts turned to the money you have or the money you lack, at least to some degree. A good friend of mine once said, *"Money doesn't make the world go round but it certainly helps pay for the trip,"* and how true is that?

During my years as a financial planner, most of my clients were consumed with the subject of money. Virtually all of them ended up telling me the same thing in one way or another; *"Kip,*

I don't feel like I've saved enough money or invested it as wisely as I should have." Underneath it all, their real fear was that they'd either outlive their money or never have enough, no matter how much wealth they acquired. But was their definition of wealth really accurate? How do YOU define wealth? Consider the following question and then write down the answer. On a scale of one to ten, with ten being the best, how wealthy do you feel? Do you have your answer? Good.

Now, I'd like to get you to rethink your personal definition of wealth by reframing the question. What's an eye worth to you? What would you take if I offered to buy a lung or one of your hands or feet? Think about your family, your friendships, and the many blessings you experience in the course of a normal day. Taking all those things into consideration, how would you rate your wealth on that same one to ten scale? Did your estimation of your total wealth just make a radical shift? I've found that most people raise their rating a full 20-30% higher when the question is posed this way. For most people this is a major wake up call. I know it was for me the first time I was asked to perform this exercise.

I grew up in a family that always struggled with money, but the love and support was always there. I was blessed to have two grandmothers that were both saints. As their first-born grandson, they doted over me and made me feel like I could accomplish anything, just as my Mom did. It's for these reasons that I always felt wealthy even though we had little financial wealth. This was my first introduction to the real definition of wealth. I'm convinced that love is the most important thing we can teach (and give) to our children. From love we gain the confidence and courage we need to tackle any challenge that comes our way in life. Cindy and I were both incredibly fortunate to have been raised in an environment of unconditional love, and it's the kind of environment we strive to create in our own home.

Does your definition of wealth come with an expectation that life is going to be problem-free? If so, you're in for another wake up call. Wealthy people encounter obstacles in life just like everyone else does. What sets the truly successful folks apart from the ones who barely get by is how they respond to life's setbacks. You can't always control the events in your life, but you can always control your response to them – you always have a choice. Napoleon Hill repeats this idea several times in *Think and Grow Rich*, saying that every adversity carries within it the seed of an equal or greater benefit. Successful people train themselves to recognize and act on these opportunities, even when the events that bring them look and feel like defeats at first.

One lesson I learned that drove this message home for me is that parents can't be expected to be perfect. I never met my real father and was adopted by my mother's second husband. She gave birth to me when she was only 18 years old and sacrificed a great deal by bringing me into the world. Instead of being free to enjoy life as a young adult without responsibilities, she was forced to raise a kid while she was still one herself. She could have focused on how tough it was to be a single mother at that age. Instead, she worked hard to become a nurse, and I've always admired her unstoppable energy and work ethic.

Are you watching for the opportunities that come your way disguised as problems? I love what I do and each day is an exciting learning experience. The up times are always great, but everything I've really learned in life in a deep, internal way seems to have come from my tough times – the valleys versus the peaks. Have you ever wondered why so many important deals get made on the golf course? Sure, the camaraderie's great and the amenities are nice, but there's a lot more to it than competition or prestige. You can learn a lot about someone's character by the way they respond when they're having a bad game. Life is like that too. Some people fold under pressure. Others focus. You have a choice today – which kind of person do you want to be?

When people ask me about the secret to my own success, I love to talk about the values we've covered in this chapter, but I especially enjoy talking about the wealth-building magic of being an entrepreneur. There's a special satisfaction in knowing that you're free to achieve success as YOU define it and do it on your own terms. While the experience isn't for everyone, many of us are just born with entrepreneurial instincts and I don't know of a better way to build massive wealth. Entrepreneurs are willing to think independently, take informed risks and enjoy the rewards that come from living close to the edge. When you're an entrepreneur, adrenaline is your friend! Even failure can be enjoyable, especially when you can look in the rearview mirror and realize how much you've learned from it.

As you've figured out by now, I didn't come from a country club family, so when I began my Wall Street career, fitting in didn't come naturally to me. After a few years, though, I discovered that I not only belonged but also that I brought a work ethic to the table that enabled me to surpass the successes of most of my peers; even those who were born into great wealth. Looking back on the experience, I wouldn't change a thing. In fact, I'm convinced that being born into money can actually be a disadvantage. I would never have learned how much fun it could be to become a self-made multimillionaire. Here's the best news of all – you don't have to just take my word for it. You can do it too and find out for yourself!

CHAPTER TWELVE
CRASHPROOF
PROSPERITY

As I've been saying for a very long time, the real keys to turning the economy around are reaching a true floor in employment, the housing market and "honestly" re-engaging the American consumer, whose purchasing power is responsible for over 70% of our nation's GDP. In turn, these changes will reverse rapidly deteriorating corporate profits. In this chapter, you and I are now going to examine *Crashproof Prosperity* from two interdependent perspectives (everything's connected). First, we'll look at the macro level policy changes that must take place to pull our government and financial institutions back from the brink of total collapse. Second, we'll walk through a powerful list of micro level changes you can begin making TODAY to ensure that you and the people you care about are on the receiving end of the greatest transfer of wealth in recorded history.

This is my five step plan to reverse America's path to economic destruction on a dime. Once implemented, these steps have the power to turn the economy around in less than one year. I'm talking about a reversal from what economists are predicting will be a barely positive GDP to a long-term 5-8% GDP beginning in under 12 months. Does this sound too good to be true? It's not − read on.

Step One: Eliminate all Federal taxes for one full year, both personal and business. This first step is far and away the most important, and will result in an immediate explosion of true economic growth. Yes, this will result in approximately $2 trillion less in government tax receipts, but isn't this about the same size as Obama's stimulus package, which also resulted in "real" tax liabilities for which our children and grandchildren will be on the hook for decades to come? 100% of my *real* $2 trillion stimulus would work its way into the economy immediately. Also remember that 30 cents of every government stimulus dollar is lost in administrative costs, fraud and bureaucratic red tape. My plan would have ZERO administrative costs, hence an additional $600 billion in growth.

There's no better way to stimulate consumer spending and business hiring than with direct and immediate tax cuts. Recall from an earlier chapter that we lost our manufacturing economy long ago, and it was replaced by a consumer-based economy. Therefore, in order to turn the economy around we must see the return of a true manufacturing base, which can once again be accomplished with a vast reduction in the power of labor unions and government red tape and bureaucracy. With these courageous moves the American consumer would return faster than Bernanke can say "I'm really just a college professor." The velocity of money (which has been essentially nonexistent) would return overnight and the failed policies of the FED and Keynesian economists would very quickly become a thing of the past.

In addition, the Federal government should mandate that all 50 states do the same with state sales taxes. The increased spending by consumers would quickly shore up housing and retail spending, which in turn would boost employment by five million jobs in year one alone, hence restoring the American consumer's rightful place in our troubled economy. Who knows, America may even return to being a nation of savers, rather than a nation of spenders. Bankrupt states such as California, New York, Illinois and Michigan (along with the other 40 or so) would soon be talking about the economic miracle they're witnessing right before their eyes, and the tent cities that are springing up throughout the country would vanish. The $2 trillion in Federal tax savings, along with the tax savings in all 50 states, would go directly into our bank accounts and the result would be a near overnight return to prosperity across the country. When foreign governments see the incredible turnaround happening here they'll launch similar initiatives, and any fears of Great Depression 2 (or the Greater Depression) could be a distant memory. And here's the real key: Once the country witnessed this *American Miracle*, even Keynesians would be forced to admit – once and for all – that allowing a hard working population to keep more of their income results in massive economic growth; just as JFK, Reagan, Clinton and Bush II learned during their presidencies.

Step Two: Cut the Federal Government's Budget by 25%. Make these changes effective immediately and across the board. This mandate will send a strong message that government is indeed serious about reducing our exploding national debt. Regardless of what the *official* government figures may tell us, we've been in this recession for over 3 years. Incredibly however, if you were to exclude the counterfeit growth that came almost entirely from mortgage equity withdrawals from 2002 on, the hard reality is that the US has now been in a recession for almost 10 years. What is equally incredible is that even in light of these Depressionary statistics, we have yet to see *any* reduction in the size of the Federal and state governments – in fact until 2011 they have continued to grow each and every year by 3% on average.

Here's the bottom line when it comes to our level of government spending; when you factor in entitlements, total debt is now more than $100 trillion and unless we address this problem immediately, taxes will have to rise to 70% on all Americans within the next 10 years, and that will be just to pay the interest due. And unfortunately, I'm being generous with the 10 year estimate – especially when foreigners stop buying our debt and the FED implodes on itself. So, let's get started now. The positive message that the Federal government will send with these budget cuts will result in restored trust globally and trickle down to states and to individual families – again, overnight.

Step Three: Place the US dollar (and hopefully all currencies around the world) back on the gold Standard. President Richard M. Nixon removed what was left of the gold standard in 1971, resulting in the debasement of our currency and massive inflation. If you've ever wondered why both spouses in a typical family must work full time just to have the same standard of living that one income provided just 30 years ago, look no further than the FED, central banks globally, and the resulting debasement of currencies around the world. Yet, at the same time, one ounce of gold today will still purchase almost exactly what it did 10, 30, 50, 100, 500 and 1000 years ago. Let this fact sink in for a moment. When it really hits home you will then have a complete understanding of the poison of central banks, the global cartel of bankers they make wealthy, and fiat currency inflation. A country cannot thrive with a fiat currency – end of story – which is why ALL fiat currencies in history have ultimately returned to their intrinsic value. Yes, paper.

My plan to begin a 20 year incremental policy to back each dollar by 20% in gold (1% per year) may seem simplistic, but I have yet to find anyone make a valid argument as to why it would not work. Sure, I understand the supply/demand dynamics brought on by a limited supply of gold, and frankly therein lies the beauty. This move would force the government to turn off the printing presses for the US dollar. Simply put, we would not be able to print what we do not have in gold reserves. This would force the government to balance the budget, just as each business and family must. Exactly how could that be bad policy?

Step Four: Limit the influence of lobbyists and special interest groups with radical reforms, including outlawing the ability to become a lobbyist once you have served in public office. Insider dealings and conflicts of interest will ultimately destroy the US, just as they did during the Roman Empire, and as they're currently doing on Wall Street. Multinational corporations have quietly bypassed our representative form of government by using lobbyists to purchase influence through campaign contributions and other special favors to the politicians who care more about re-election and the transfer of wealth (from voters to the elected) than public service. Our system is imploding from within, and we must take immediate steps to restore honesty and transparency to our legislative process. Wayne Allyn Root has some powerful recommendations in this area, and I back his ideology 100%.

Step Five: Abolish the vast majority of financial derivatives. Eliminate the ability to create or to use the vast majority of derivative instruments in the financial industry — especially those that do not verifiably add to the well-being and health of a particular industry or commodity. Even Warren Buffet's own Berkshire Hathaway empire suffered record losses when he gambled on the same type of derivative instruments he once called "weapons of mass financial destruction." Derivatives make a lot of sense for a farmer that is hedging against a bad crop season, but they make no sense when used by financial institutions to increase their leverage by 100% while placing the entire financial system as we know it at risk. Unless this $700 trillion, mostly unregulated industry is transformed for the good, it is only a matter of time before the entire financial system as we know it implodes in on itself, taking us all down with it.

This Five Step Plan is not meant to be a thesis paper – instead, it's a blueprint for returning the US to being the global power that it once was. These actions will restore economic security and if acted on sooner than later, have the ability to reverse the risk of another Great Depression. Remember, if our leaders in Washington really believed that Obama's $1 trillion jobs program would create 4 million new jobs, then we could simply throw $2 trillion into the program to create 8 million new jobs. Or, why not $3 trillion to create 12 million new jobs? Folks, these government sponsored job programs simply do not work as advertised. They're simply a thinly veiled excuse to increase the size and power of Washington and its shadowy clique of unelected power brokers.

Bigger government is not the answer; government-created jobs are not the answer; trillions in taxpayer-funded bailouts are not the answer. The business model of the entire financial system is broken and without decisive intervention, the pain is only going to get worse. Trillions are being spent by the government on bailout after bailout, yet the economy continues to fade away. The historically symbolic Obama presidency that began with "the audacity of hope" is rapidly dissolving into an era of disappointment and fear as leading Democrats openly break ranks with their own party line and question key components of the administration's economic stimulus program.

Will these ideas find a champion among our elected representatives? That remains to be seen, but time is running out. Texas Congressman Ron Paul, Kentucky Senator Rand Paul (Ron Paul's son) and Libertarian National Congressional Committee Chairman Wayne Allyn Root are three voices of reason that can make a real difference, but they need our help and we need more like them at all levels of government. It's going to take a critical mass of integrity-based fiscal conservatism, both in Washington and among the voting public to eliminate fiat currency, reverse the national debt spiral and hold the Federal Reserve accountable to the American people until we're able to abolish the evils of central banking once and for all. As a free nation we can and must seize true constitutional control back from the private profiteers who have hijacked the US economy and along with it the financial destinies of our children and grandchildren.

Even if we do succeed in bringing sanity back to our government and financial institutions and reversing some of their failed economic policies, it pains me to tell you that *it's already too late to escape many of the consequences.* In the very near future, a lot of good people are going to have to weather some tough lifestyle changes and a painful deleveraging process. The only question is whether this correction will be allowed to happen naturally, or whether short-sighted government intervention will continue to prolong and deepen it, as it did during the first Great Depression. With all this in mind, it should be clear to you by now that top-down policy changes can only be a part of the solution. No matter how level or tilted the playing field may be, creating true *Crashproof Prosperity* won't be possible without individual responsibility to take informed action.

In speaking with my VRA subscribers and the WMI member community around the world, I often hear something like this; *"I know that it takes money to make money, but right now I just don't have any."* Regardless of where you may be financially, the most important thing to remember is that virtually everyone who has achieved financial independence had little or no money at some point in their lives – and some more than once! It might surprise you to learn this, but studies show that more than 80% of today's millionaires are not only self-made, but also came from some kind of limited financial background. So, what's the one common denominator that the wealthy have in common? What's the single thing they can all point to as the secret to their financial success?

Simply put, the wealthy became that way because they found one thing and stuck with it, no matter what. It's the quality of perseverance, or as Wayne Allyn Root put it in the last chapter, being RELENTLESS! Too many times we jump from one thing to another, always hoping that the grass will be greener on the other side, and it rarely is. Instead, if we make a decision to give 100% to one thing – whatever that one thing may be – and to never give up, regardless of any obstacles or challenges in our way, it must inevitably follow that we'll begin to see financial success and ultimately, experience true financial freedom.

While this rarely happens overnight (nothing lasting ever does), measurable success will begin to manifest very, very quickly. Then, by following the core principles like the ones found in WMI's 1% Solution, you'll begin to experience exponential wealth creation. At first, it will appear in your daily mindset, and then it will manifest in your bank and investment accounts. Depending on your commitment level, you should know that all of this can take place in an incredibly short period of time!

Think about it this way; are you willing to apply yourself 100% for the next three to five years in order to experience a lifetime of financial freedom? If the answer is yes, then make the decision TODAY to get started. Then, treat every day as a new day of opportunity and keep the past where it belongs – in the past. Your perseverance will grow with each passing day and after the first 30 days, you'll have formed new and exciting habits that will help to keep you moving forward on the path to success. I look forward to seeing you at the top!

As I've said many times, more millionaires were created coming out of the Great Depression than existed in the entire world before the crash. $50 trillion has already begun moving from the uninformed to the informed and by the time it's done we'll have all witnessed the greatest transfer of wealth in history. The bad news is that extremely tough times are ahead for those on the losing side. The good news is that by educating yourself, sticking relentlessly to an intelligent plan and taking decisive, contrarian action, you can ensure that you and your loved ones are will be on the receiving end of this historic wealth transfer.

Once in every two to three generations an opportunity presents itself that enables those who are prepared for it to become wealthy beyond their wildest dreams – generational wealth that passes from your children to their children and on and on. The events that began unfolding in 2008 represent this once in a lifetime opportunity and those who act on it over the next three years will be the major beneficiaries. If you want to be one of them here's what to do.

One; educate yourself and become a critical thinker. There are a small handful of economists and market analysts I trust and I've made a habit of surrounding myself with the brightest and most integrity-driven minds in the world of finance. I've mentioned several of them in this book. When I suggest that people emulate their contrarian approach to investing, I'm not talking about adopting a careless or reckless attitude about money. Quite the opposite, in fact. In order to make good financial judgments, you've got to be able to think critically and question the status quo, and you can't do that without reliable information.

The challenge we all face is knowing which information sources to trust and how to sort out fact from fiction. I'll tell you right now that by the time you read about a "trend" in the main stream media, the truly wealthy have already made their plays and moved on to the next big opportunity. For over 15 years I was a Financial Advisor and Vice President of Investments for two of the most respected firms on Wall Street. Sadly, this experience taught me that the quickest and easiest way to lose money for my clients (and myself) was to follow the advice of investment firms and their research departments – to purchase or sell securities based on their marketing recommendations.

This statement probably doesn't surprise you, as over the last several years the public has learned about the vast conflicts of interest that continue to be inherent on the "street," compounded by a media machine that's dominated by many of the same multinational corporations. These conflicts make it very difficult for the average person to make money with a financial advisor. This environment forced me to learn how to analyze companies, identify industry momentum, do my own real research and develop strong relationships, proprietary screens, analysis techniques, and most importantly, to personally get to know the management teams of exciting growth companies.

To be specific, I'm speaking primarily about small and mid-cap companies ("cap" meaning the total amount of capitalization behind them). I'll consider a large cap if the situation warrants it, but small to mid-cap stocks is where the real potential lies. It's companies of this size (with market caps of $100 million to $1 billion or so), where investors can make real money in the stock market. When I say *real money*, I'm talking about annualized returns of over 50-100% per year. Sound aggressive? Too good to be true? Well, it is aggressive, but it's also completely possible.

That's why the majority of people invest in stocks – they want the opportunity to increase their net worth dramatically while having a measured degree of risk. It's all about risk versus reward. This is exactly what the Vertical Research Advisory (VRA) newsletter provides.

So, how is this accomplished, and how do we select our stocks? A significant amount of research has been done over the last 20 years in order to perfect the system of stock selection and the research is exhaustive. After a company has been selected as an interesting possibility (we speak with hundreds of company insiders and industry experts each year), we then begin a two-pronged approach. While we're speaking and meeting with the company's top insiders, we're also researching their competitors, carefully analyzing SEC filings, and using proprietary fundamental and technical screens. This approach allows us to uncover companies that fly under the radar screen of most Wall Street analysts (who operate largely based on what a company will pay in investment banking fees) and mutual fund managers.

Ideally, we enter a stock anywhere from one to three months before it's "discovered" by Wall Street and the global markets. Current VRA subscribers are updated on a regular basis with news, proprietary analysis, or a rating change on recommended companies. Once we recommend a stock, you'll want to purchase shares in the company immediately. The timing is crucial and it's important that you have a brokerage account, ideally an online account you have control over and one that features low fees and strong account management features. Many VRA subscribers use services like E*TRADE, Ameritrade, Fidelity or Schwab. It's also very important to follow proper account management and diversification principles. Please remember to take equal positions in each stock, and never "load the boat" or put all your eggs in one basket.

In my former career as a money manager and financial advisor, it was extremely troubling to me that I was only able to help a few high-net-worth individuals with their monetary goals. I was searching for something that would level the playing field and give the average person the power to control their financial destiny. That's why I created the VRA — to connect my subscribers with the potential for unprecedented investment returns by following fundamentals that everyone should know. You can learn more about it at www.vraletter.com.

Two; become an entrepreneur. If you read my previous book with Karl Bessey, *Two Roads, One Journey*, you already know that there have always been two parallel financial systems at work in the world — a "wage" system for workers and a "profit" system for owners. During an interview about his world famous *Cabo Wabo®* tequila and theme cantina empire, rocker Sammy Hagar is rumored to have said, *"I don't endorse — I own!"* The only way to create massive and lasting wealth (while you're still young enough to enjoy it) is to get yourself out of the wage system and into the profit system. The best and only way I know to do that is to tap your entrepreneurial spirit and start a business of your own. Jack Canfield likes to say that if you don't have a plan, you'll end up working for someone who does!

Why am I so passionate about entrepreneurship as the way out of the economic turmoil we're in? When confronted with a crisis, it's not uncommon for people to have knee-jerk reactions that end up doing more harm than good. The disgust with Washington, Wall Street, and Corporate America has people questioning (to put it mildly) ethics, policies, and how we could have allowed a mess like this to happen in the first place. I'm convinced that we'll look back five years from now and see that the worst economic period since the Great Depression resulted in a sea-change in the way business is done and that the perception of Corporate America and the Government will be forever changed.

Gone will be the days when people trust others to determine the fate of their finances, their careers, and their future. Personal accountability and responsibility will replace the malaise that has permeated our culture over the last two decades, and with this evolution will come a new found sense of personal pride and self-reliance. It's in this kind of environment that an entrepreneur thrives and it's why I believe that the way of thinking I've described in *Crashproof* will ultimately help millions to achieve more than they ever thought possible.

Small businesses create the vast majority of jobs in our economy and also generate most of the tax revenues that keep this country going. These courageous companies represent the kind of growth, innovation and creativity that made America great. That's all wonderful, but the obvious barrier to entry the average person faces, especially today, is that most don't have top secret plans for the next big computer breakthrough, or hundreds of thousands in startup capital for buildings and equipment or a turnkey national franchise of some sort. Most need something they can do part time while they work another job (if they're lucky enough to still have one) or start on a shoestring from home. This is why I'm a huge believer in the self-determination that's made possible through the direct sales and network marketing industries.

It was precisely this vision that led me and my partner Karl Bessey to create Wealth Masters International. Our dream was to form a wealth creation community, populated by independent entrepreneurs who have a desire to create wealth in others through financial education, combined with a solid grounding in wellness and personal development principles. We're convinced that this unique combination of Wealth, Health and Wisdom is the secret to the explosive growth we've experienced since we first planted our own contrarian flag in the financial world back in 2005.

We're now expanding rapidly in over 100 countries, with a goal of becoming a billion dollar public company and an IPO, with one of the most innovative and lucrative compensation plans in the history of direct marketing. Our business model is based on trust and creating success and wealth in others – the very definition of abundance as we see it. If you're not already with us, we'd love for you to see what we're all about and consider becoming a part of the WMI family because the success stories I hear every day from our member community are truly moving. We're literally changing lives for the better all over the world.

Although I'm understandably a "proud papa" when it comes to Wealth Masters, there are a number of reputable companies out there that will allow you to become an entrepreneur on your own terms and start signing your paychecks on the front instead of the back. The important thing is to choose a business that rewards you in a meaningful way for creating success in others and – this is critical – offers a product or service you truly believe in. No matter how much money you make, it won't be sustainable enough to create lasting prosperity in your life unless the work you're doing is in total alignment with your internal compass. Pick an opportunity that fits who you really are and then work it relentlessly, day in and day out.

Also make certain that the people behind the company are integrity-driven and committed to keeping the right support systems in place to ensure your long term success, not just a few short term windfalls. When Karl and I started Wealth Masters, we wanted to help everyone, in *every* area of their lives, regardless of how much or little might be in their bank accounts. This led to our holistic drive to give our worldwide WMI community unprecedented access to products, services and experiences that remove all barriers to Wealth, Health and Wisdom. Since the very beginning of WMI, we've held fast to the core principle of remaining free of both debt and conflicts of interest. That commitment continues to serve the company and our community well and we've never regretted it.

Three; recognize that precious metals are the only real currencies. It's clear to anyone who's paying attention that the US dollar, along with likely every global currency, must be printed into oblivion in order for the government to continue funding its $100 trillion in total debt. There's only one path for the US dollar, short-term and long-term, and that path is straight down. This is the major point I've been making about the inflation/deflation debate for the last few of years. It doesn't matter whether we have inflation or deflation in academic economist's terms, because we're guaranteed to have *currency inflation*, which means that precious metal prices must continue to rocket skyward.

This is the first time I've published my personal price target for gold outside of the WMI and VRA community, but here it is; $10,200/ounce. And I wouldn't be surprised to see silver trade all the way up to $200/ounce before this hyperinflationary era is over. If you think these price targets are outrageous, many of the world's top precious metals experts – some of which are in my personal mastermind group – have price targets that make mine look tame by comparison. Remember, gold rose by several trillion percent during Weimar Germany's currency collapse! Timing is the question of course, but it's most likely that we'll reach these prices in three to eight years. If you're not a VRA subscriber, you should know that I've been recommending gold since it was below $300/ounce and silver since it was about $5/ounce. We're in only the third inning or so of this ball game (which will likely go into extra innings) so an essential *Crashproof Prosperity* strategy is to either *continue* buying precious metals or *get started* buying gold and silver *immediately*.

Vital point; make sure that the precious metals dealer you work with is respected and checks out fully, with a clean business record of more than10 years. As with any bull market, like the incredible one we've seen in gold and silver (40%+ per year for close to nine years), scam artists come out of the woodwork to prey on unknowing investors. Recently, there have been reports of gold plated *"tungsten"* coins/bars masquerading as *pure* gold coins/bars. In addition, you should not pay more than about 1% over spot price, and delivery should be made within no more than two weeks.

Recently, there have been some emerging opportunities to get positioned in precious metals without the logistical problems or risks associated with having to hold the physical gold and silver; however these carry some degree of risk as well, such as loss of privacy and dependence on the company that holds your gold/silver. More on this type of strategy will be announced at Wealth Masters events and in my VRA updates in the months to come, but I strongly encourage you to keep your eyes open for these and do your own research in the meantime. Also, please remember *The Golden Rule; he who owns the gold rules*. And this; once precious metals really begin to take off, the fewer people that know about yours, the better!

In addition, a select number of mining stocks with specific performance characteristics are an excellent way to invest in the precious metals space, but again I caution you to distribute your investments proportionally rather than getting too aggressive with just one opportunity. My last VRA recommendation in this industry rose more than 1400% in price, but as great as that may have been; owning just one stock is akin to taking all of your money to Las Vegas and putting it on black – in other words, not recommended.

Importantly, as fiat currency based hyperinflation continues to build, there will also be extraordinary opportunities in the energy industry, specifically oil and natural gas. While I continue to wait for a form of alternative energy that truly excites me (and no, wind and solar are not it), we will continue to see oil and gas prices in or around the three figure area. This presents dramatic upside potential for select, small cap exploration and production companies with strong management and large exploration licenses, specifically outside of the US. Worst case, the gains you make in these kinds of investments can help to offset the increased price we'll be forced to pay for energy, or best case, possibly even create the next Rockefeller.

Finally, begin researching and developing relationships for long term food storage products and community co-ops for vegetable and fruit crops. WMI is actively researching this industry and plans to have specific recommendations in the very near future. As uncomfortable as this thought might be, one of the most painful ways the public is harmed in a hyperinflationary environment is through dramatic increases in food prices – in fact we're witnessing the early stages of this process today. Be prepared just in case!

Four; cut your exposure to any form of government-backed securities, including Treasury and Municipal bonds. Due to skyrocketing monetary inflation (which will be a direct result of the crash of fiat currencies like the US dollar and sharply higher interest rates), US Treasury Bonds are going to get absolutely hammered. Like a see-saw, bond prices fall as interest rates rise, and due to the insane monetary decisions from our leaders in Washington and Bernanke at the FED, our government bonds are going drop like a rock in the coming years. But don't just take my word for it. Julian Robertson, one of the all time money making greats, is convinced that the US dollar will become so weak that the central banks of China and Japan will stop purchasing Treasuries altogether. You should know that as founder of the investment firm Tiger Management, Robertson turned $8 million in start-up capital in 1980 into $22 billion by the late 1990s.

Back in January of 2008, Robertson told Fortune, *"I've made a big bet on it. I really think I'm going to make 20 or 30 times on my money."* This is definitely one of Robertson's trademark 'bet the farm' plays if there ever was one. In a recent interview with Value Investor Insight, Robertson lays out further rationale for his play. He says, *"I'm amazed at the amount of money the government is throwing at this thing. You don't even react anymore unless somebody's talking about $1 trillion. I genuinely admire the administration's courage in doing what it's doing, but not the wisdom of it. I look at the TALF (Term Asset-Backed Securities Loan Facility) program, for example, and it's almost a bribe to get people to put on more leverage. I ask anyone to give me an example of an economy beefed up by huge amounts of quantitative easing that did not inflate tremendously when or if the economy improved. I think what we're doing now will either fail, or it will result in unbelievably high inflation, and tragically, maybe both. That would mean a depression and explosive inflation, which is frightening."*

While the outcome he describes may be frightening, it's the exact scenario that Robertson is wagering on. He's convinced, with good reason, that the US has not solved the current problems and that things are going to go from bad to really bad. He likened the current US situation to that of Japan in 1989, except that we're in far worse shape. For those that remember the late 1970s and early 1980s when interest rates and inflation were at 15-20%, this is the forecast that lots of smart money people are making right now. The FED is keeping interest rates at ridiculously low levels to keep the economy from going over a cliff, but this amazingly short-sighted approach will wind up completely bankrupting our already diluted fiat currency. When the dollar begins its crash, rates will scream higher and there will be nothing that the FED can do about it.

What I'm describing to you is called the "Armageddon" trade, a staple recommendation of the VRA. One of the major risks in becoming the "bailout nation" is that the trillions upon trillions being spent to supposedly save our economy from completely imploding will in fact turn out to be disastrous for inflation rates and the prices of US Treasury bonds (as well as all global government debt). I've touched on this already in an earlier chapter, but it's important to underscore the idea one more time; as we continue to issue record amounts of new debt to pay for massive government obligations, who will actually buy our country's bonds? The answer is that almost no one will be willing to buy them, and certainly not at the current yields. The Chinese have stopped buying (and are quietly selling), the Japanese have their own debt problems to deal with (they are close to Zimbabwe levels now) and our friends in the Middle East are busy bailing out their artificial empire that they call an emerging economy.

All of this background explains why I refer to shorting government bonds and the dollar as the "Armageddon" trade. This strategy will soar in value as the US economy falls deeper into recession/depression and hyperinflation. In fact, the actions of our government and Federal Reserve practically guarantee it. Make no mistake about it, folks – this is another very real bubble that's infinitely bigger than the credit and housing bubbles that came before it. And it's going to pop. When it bursts, it's going to burst wide open and with it, we will have much higher interest rates and inflation. Warren Buffet has warned about the same thing, with both he and Robertson saying that we could have the late 1970s all over again. For those that do not subscribe to the VRA, please consult your broker. This strategy is not for the faint of heart, and it is also simply not possible to describe fully in this book. By the way, this last statement does not mean that the strategy is difficult to use or to understand, simply that the purpose of this book is not to provide individual stock or bond recommendations – rather, it's to empower you with the insights to employ these strategies on your own – as an independent-minded contrarian.

Because you've invested in yourself by reading this book, you've now been given a choice to become a part of a very small and exclusive group of well-informed future millionaires and billionaires. Whether you act on that opportunity and follow these recommendations while there's still time is up to you. So, what does this mean for us? Massive opportunity! For all the reasons I've outlined for you in this book, I believe that the coming Depression – if it plays out the way the indicators are telling me it will – will be far worse than anything we experienced in the 1930s. With each passing day, the writing is on the wall for all to see. To sum up everything we've talked about at a glance, here's how to build *Crashproof Prosperity* into your life and prepare for the turbulent times ahead:

> *One:* Eliminate as much personal debt as possible. If this means selling your home and renting, then so be it. Because home prices could drop as much as 30-50% from current levels you could be doing yourself a big favor in the long run.

> *Two:* Live beneath your means, and have this important discussion with your family – immediately. I know this may seem depressing, but if it means that you survive and have a roof over your head, it will turn out to be the best family meeting you ever had.

> *Three:* Sell all investments in the stock market, except carefully researched individual stocks that go up in price as the overall market goes down.

> *Four:* Instead of "old paradigm" securities, buy gold and silver. Consider this; the amount you make in precious metals over the next five years might

allow you to buy an entire city block in the years to come.

Five: At the risk of being embarrassed in the event you're wrong, tell everyone you care about – friends and family – about your plan so that they can begin doing the same things.

And herein lies one of the most powerful, multi-generational wealth accumulation strategies behind these five steps. Those that prepare for the financial wreckage on its way will be positioned perfectly to buy *real* assets at 20-30 year lows, likely within the next three years. Imagine buying your ideal piece of property at 50% below current prices, or buying your favorite blue chip stocks at a 70% markdown on today's quotes. And how about this; imagine selling your gold and silver at a 500% premium over today's prices in order to make these very purchases! This is what being a new paradigm thinker – an independently minded contrarian – is all about.

I have to tell you honestly that I greet every single day with gratitude. My life experiences have afforded me the opportunity to pursue a mission in life that truly inspires me – *to create success and wealth in others.* It's an adventure in the grandest sense of that word and the thrill of watching it unfold in lives all over the world will never wear off. The words "success" and "wealth" mean different things to different people. For some, it might simply mean seeing a light at the end of the tunnel; a monthly cash flow increase of $500; credit card debts paid off within just a few months; a big enough credit score increase to allow a complete restructuring of all debts with more favorable interest rates and lower payments.

For others, success might mean the peace of mind that comes from taking charge as your own "trusted financial advisor" so you can successfully watch your own back. No matter how you define success, be it time freedom, money freedom or some other kind of personal fulfillment, the most important thing is being empowered to create it and live it on your own terms. I know that many readers share a similar past to mine. Maybe you've reached this point in your life and find yourself asking, *"is this it – am I doing what I was meant to do?"* Obviously, you're the only one who can answer that question. All I can tell you is that it's no accident that you and I have found each other and that you're reading this book. I know this as an absolute certainty. Everything's connected and everything happens for a reason.

Maybe your future will include a seven-figure-plus bank account. Maybe you're meant to empower others with the *Crashproof Prosperity* message as they become entrepreneurs and take charge of their lives. Maybe your destiny is to experience abundance in the form of more satisfying relationships, better quality of life or more vibrant wellness. Perhaps you dream of massive generational wealth that you can pass on to your children and to their children – we're living in a rare point in history where it's genuinely possible! Launch that business, that charitable outreach, that book, that movie, that painting, that symphony that's waiting inside of you. Whatever your passion is, the world needs it. My desire for you, and the reason I wrote this book with *you* in mind, is to see *all* of these things and more become a reality for you as YOU choose to envision them. That's the essence of what *Crashproof Prosperity* is all about. Now that you know the truth, what are you going to do with it?

FOR FURTHER STUDY

America's Great Depression – Murray Rothbard

Atlas Shrugged – Ayn Rand

Bonfire of the Vanities – Tom Wolfe

FDR's Folly – Jim Powell

Guide to Investing in Gold and Silver – Michael Maloney

Hoodwinked – John Perkins

I.O.U.S.A. – (documentary film) Patrick Creadon, Director

Revolution – Ron Paul

The Arms of Krupp – William Manchester

The Conscience of a Libertarian – Wayne Allyn Root

The Creature from Jekyll Island – G. Edward Griffin

The Trends Journal – Gerald Celente

Think and Grow Rich – Napoleon Hill

Two Roads, One Journey – Kip Herriage & Karl Bessey

Vertical Research Advisory Investment Newsletter – Kip Herriage

ACKNOWLEDGEMENTS

No labor of love, like this book, the Vertical Research Advisory newsletter, or the Wealth Masters International vision, can succeed without the tireless support of countless individuals who share our commitment to create wealth and success in others. I want to convey my sincere thanks to the people who have helped to make *Crashproof Prosperity* a reality, not just in print, but more importantly, in the lives of the worldwide Wealth Masters community and my loyal family of VRA subscribers.

Carol Mott (my mom), for your unconditional love and unstoppable work ethic. Love ya mom. Ken Herriage (my adopted father) — another great role model. He worked two jobs to make sure that my mom could stay home with my two sisters Susan and Marla and me. David and Patricia Talbot, for having such an amazing daughter and for proving that in-laws can be great friends as well.

Wayne Allyn Root, for teaching me how to be relentless. It's kinda cool knowing the future President of the United States as well. Deanna Latson, for your true friendship and genuine compassion for others. 2011 is going to be the start of something big. Mary Dee Bell – you're my "right hand woman." Can you believe how fast the last eleven years have flown by? You make what I do easy and you are an absolute true friend. Love ya girl. Michael Hamburger – Hammy, your energy makes all the difference. Thanks for your work ethic, your integrity and your willingness to go the extra mile. Bobby Bell – In quietness and confidence shall be your strength. This quote from the bible sums up my thoughts about the way you walk the talk. Appreciate you! Morgan Johnson – love your professionalism and gentle spirit. You do a wonderful job of keeping your arms around all of our day to day operations. The real deal. Andy Allen – my best friend since we were 6. My original brother from another mother. Love ya man.

Karl Bessey – what can I say? You're the best business partner a guy could ever have. Salt of the earth. Let's take this thing to a billion together and help millions along the way. Tyler and Sam – you boys make life a fantastic adventure every day. I can't wait to see where your lives will take you and couldn't be more proud of you and of the young men you've become. I love you guys! And most importantly, to my wife Cindy – thanks for making me the happiest man on the planet for 22 years. I can't wait to see where the future will take us. I love you Shook!

- Kip Herriage

ABOUT THE AUTHOR

Kip Herriage is the CEO and Co-Founder of Wealth Masters International and the Founder and Editor of the top-performing Vertical Research Advisory Newsletter, subscribed to by savvy investors worldwide. His economic forecasts and predictions over the years have earned him the nickname "The Nostradamus of Investing". Kip also proudly serves on the board of the Libertarian National Congressional Committee (LNCC). Prior to forming Wealth Masters, Kip spent over 15 years as Vice President, Financial Planner and Money Manager for two of the largest investment firms on Wall Street where he managed over $70 million for his clients. During his tenure, Kip became known as one of the premiere financial minds in the industry, offering trusted guidance to his valued clients.

For Kip, success came easy early on as his financial prowess cemented him as a prominent fixture on Wall Street. However, with great success came a heavy toll. 60+ hour work weeks, two hour commutes each day, and most taxing of all, precious moments spent away from his family; Cindy, Kip's wife of 21 years and his two sons Tyler and Sam. Kip recalls, *"This was not my idea of the American Dream and was certainly not the way I wanted to be remembered as a father by my two sons. In addition, I always knew that there was an entrepreneur inside of me just waiting for the right opportunity, and at some point I knew I would have to make the move in order to achieve the true freedom that successful entrepreneurs master."*

In 1999, Kip made the decision that would forever change the course of not only his own life, but thousands of other lives around the world. He retired from Wall Street at the age of 38, took his expertise and accolades and moved on. *"As I entered the world of an independent financial advisor, I began to receive invitations to attend events sponsored by network marketing organizations, and I immediately recognized how like-minded and passionate these high-energy entrepreneurs were. I also learned one of the most surprising things of all; my college degrees, licenses, and 15 years on Wall Street had actually prevented me, not helped me, from discovering many of the world's best financial strategies, top money managers, and an entire network of the brightest minds around the globe."*

Soon Kip was interacting with the world's most advanced thought leaders in finance, personal development and alternative wellness by studying their books, attending their events and working with them individually. The profound life-lesson he uncovered along the way, as Dr. Napoleon Hill says in *Think and*

Grow Rich, the #1 selling business book of all time, was this; *"Whatever the mind can conceive and believe, it can achieve."* By refusing to settle for less Kip Herriage now lives his American Dream. "As the CEO of WMI, I now have the opportunity to do something absolutely and undeniably amazing to give 110% of myself to the singular pursuit of helping others change their lives, just as I have been so fortunate to do in my own life. My hope is that everyone reading this will go to the Wealth Masters International home page and take the time to read our Business Plan, which also contains our Mission Statement. These documents are much more than just words on a page; they serve as the guide for all that we do, as we remain steadfast in our goal of providing individuals with the most powerful personal solutions in existence."

ALSO BY KIP HERRIAGE (with Karl Bessey)

In *Two Roads – One Journey*, international entrepreneurs and business leaders Kip Herriage and Karl Bessey share life-changing insights on how ordinary people can achieve extraordinary wealth. Their success stories trace the dramatically different roads these men traveled to the life of abundance they now enjoy as partners in their mission to help others experience unprecedented levels of success. You'll discover, as they did, how small habits of thought and action can lead to huge breakthroughs in wealth, health and wisdom. As this book challenges your assumptions, you'll be inspired to release your limitations and chart a new course to the life of your dreams - and beyond.

DISCLAIMER

This book is intended to provide a broad instructional overview on general economic and financial concepts and does not recommend or endorse any particular investment instruments or strategies. This information is made available with the understanding that the author and affiliated staff and business partners are not providing investment, legal or tax advice. The informational content of *Crashproof Prosperity* should not be used in place of a consultation with a professionally certified and/ or licensed practitioner and is not intended to address individual cases or financial circumstances. Liability for individual actions or omissions based upon the contents of this book is expressly disclaimed. Trademarks and trade names that may be quoted in this book are the property of their respective owners.

CPSIA information can be obtained at www.ICGtesting.com
Printed in the USA
LVOW012318261211

261141LV00008B/192/P

9 780578 073101